the 7
laws of
enough

the 7 laws of enough

CULTIVATING A LIFE OF SUSTAINABLE ABUNDANCE

Gina LaRoche *and* Jennifer Cohen

PRINCIPALS AT SEVEN STONES LEADERSHIP GROUP

Foreword by Lynne Twist

PARALLAX
PRESS

BERKELEY, CALIFORNIA

Parallax Press
P.O. Box 7355
Berkeley, CA 94707
parallax.org

Parallax Press is the publishing division of
Plum Village Community of Engaged Buddhism, Inc.

Printed in Canada
Cover design by Debbie Berne
Text design by Happenstance Type-O-Rama
Author photograph © Mistina Hanscom
Text printed on 100% post-consumer waste recycled paper

Library of Congress Cataloging-in-Publication Data

Names: LaRoche, Gina, author. | Cohen, Jennifer (Executive coach), author.
Title: The seven laws of enough / Gina LaRoche and Jennifer Cohen.
Description: Berkeley, California : Parallax Press, [2018]
Identifiers: LCCN 2018001629 (print) | LCCN 2018008290 (ebook) |
ISBN
  9781941529911 (Ebook) | ISBN 9781941529904 (trade paper)
Subjects: LCSH: Self-realization. | Spiritual life. | Sustainability.
Classification: LCC BJ1470 (ebook) | LCC BJ1470 .L37 2018 (print) | DDC
  170/.44—dc23
LC record available at https://lccn.loc.gov/2018001629

1 2 3 4 5 / 22 21 20 19 18

To Miriam Hawley. Thank you for standing for a sufficient world and gathering an incredible group of people who became known as the Boston Sufficiency Team.

This book is for you.

Contents

foreword

The Seven Laws of Enough invites you to explore the nourishing wellspring of *enough*. By connecting us to the taproot of sustainable abundance, Gina LaRoche and Jennifer Cohen offer each of us the opportunity to feel strong, whole, blessed, at ease, and able to rest in the profound fullness of life itself.

This book is a powerful pathway to the life we all dream of.

In order to find our way to this blissful outcome, Gina and Jennifer first wisely plunge us into awareness of the "myths of scarcity," a set of unconscious, unexamined assumptions that govern our lives without us even knowing it. They show us how we live in a consumer society that promotes the cultural conditioning and pervasive mind-set of "scarcity." This mind-set makes us believe that we are unworthy or "less than" until we acquire *more* of anything and everything. We find ourselves lost in the treacherous terrain of scarcity, constantly vying for more but never feeling that more is the "enough" we are hoping for.

All the while, the source of "enough" or "sufficiency" and a life of sustainable abundance is within our grasp—waiting patiently for our attention.

Delving in to a body of distinctions created by my own mentor, Buckminster Fuller, years ago, and developed and practiced powerfully by the Hunger Project, *The Seven Laws of Enough* lays out practices that help us orient, anchor, and find ourselves living and expressing true sufficiency, the exquisite experience of being and having enough.

Allow the message of this book to bless your life and liberate you from the tyranny of not enough time, not enough money, not enough love, not enough sleep, and the feeling of not "being" enough.

The thoughtful practices in this book will help you see how true abundance flows from enough, never from more. Follow the sound and sage words that follow and your life can be an expression of contentment, gratitude, light, and love.

Lynne Twist
October 2017

introduction

A Radical Decluttering

You are in *The Matrix*. You are offered a blue pill and a red pill. The first lets you continue on in your life as is. The second promises access to the truth about existence, the whole unadulterated truth. Which do you choose? In the *Matrix* version, the truth turns out to be that we humans are grown and harvested to feed energy to the dominating machines.

Knowing this, we probably want that blue pill. But, what if the truth is the opposite of such a sour reality? What if the truth is that everything is OK? Like, Garden of Eden OK?

It's hard to imagine. But it is the truth of sufficiency. Here are the facts: there is enough food, air, water, and other necessities for every human being on the planet to live a quality life, full of resources and abundance. In 1970, Buckminster Fuller, the architect and futurist, predicted that it would take us fifty years to see this. And, now, almost exactly fifty years later, we still haven't accepted this. Nor have we begun to organize ourselves to reflect the fact that there is enough. We believe it's time to go public with this message and to share the truth.

Here is this book in a nutshell: You are enough. You do enough. You have enough, already. If you were to orient to life, to your team, your family, and society as if that were true, we guarantee you would see life in a whole new way. You would ask different questions and frame problems differently. New solutions would emerge.

Our "modern" society is already scaring the pants off of us and making us feel bad for who we are and what we do or don't have. But fear and shame aren't conducive to positive change. To help counteract them, we'll paint a picture of what is *already* available to us. Let us peel back the layers of distortion we have grown up and been trained in and bask in the bounty available to us.

We call this bounty "sustainable abundance." Sustainable: ethical, reciprocal, just. Abundance: grateful, radiant, and present to the bounty everywhere.

As we have reflected on our own paths to living lives of sustainable abundance, we have developed a framework that we call the "Seven Laws of Enough," which offers a map of the territory ahead.

Law 1—Stories Matter. We are living in a web of stories, most of them not of our own making. We'll help you go from being stuck in your inherited stories to being the author of stories that further your life's purpose.

Law 2—I Am Enough. You are. I am. We are. When we stop questioning our birthright everything shifts.

Law 3—I Belong. Everyone does. No one has the right to tell us otherwise. We live in a culture that teaches us we're separate and has a vested interest in making us feel as if we don't belong.

Law 4—No One Is Exempt. We're set free when we accept impermanence and face what is finite and infinite. This helps us see through the lies of scarcity.

Law 5—Resting Is Required. Society encourages us to be overworked, overmedicated, overfed, undernourished, and terrified. We crave the kind of deep rest we have almost lost. We can and must reclaim it.

Law 6—Joy Is Available. We can find deep and abiding joy when we see clearly, let go of the lies, and notice what we have already.

Law 7—Love Is the Answer. This is the final law and our deepest truth. Love is the answer to the questions that plague our society and close our hearts.

Our aim for you is pure and simple: guiding you to a way of being *in* your life so you feel powerful, at ease, able to rest in life itself. When you are done reading, we hope you will know what is enough for you.

In each chapter, we will give you an opportunity to learn a new practice, to unwind from habits that no longer serve you, and connect you directly to the well of enough that's waiting for each of us.

But reading isn't enough. You must make an everyday practice of being who you wish to be, and living how you wish to live. It requires that you continually unlearn bad habits from a culture of scarcity, and persistently engage in learning new ones.

This is the gym of your life. We invite you to a lifetime membership.

Our First Workout

So here is our first practice. Gratitude, or thankfulness, provides us with an immediate and direct experience of sustainable abundance. Let's begin.

Take a deep breath and grab a pen and paper if you like.

List seven things for which you are grateful in your life right now. If seven is easy, go for fourteen. If fourteen is easy, go for twenty-one.

Now for a stretch: think of someone or something you *don't* currently feel gratitude for. Bring to mind the person or situation. Breathe and see if you can find *any* gratitude at all for the people or situation involved.

taking the scare out of scarcity

We have the power to take the "scare" out of "scarcity." We can stop buying into the myths and lies of our time. "Not enough" and "too much" are just stories that people have created—stories we can change.

What Is "Enough"?

Asking, "What is enough?" implies that you can answer the question for yourself. When you do, you've taken the first step on your own path—you can stop endlessly seeking *more*.

Enough is a declaration of something *beyond never enough. Enough* is a possibility. *Enough* is a truth. *Enough* is now. *Enough* already!

When we find ourselves dwelling in the past or worried about the future we are in a scarcity story. *Enough* is a gateway to a world where we can rest, recalibrate, and rewrite our lives.

There's not one single right definition of *enough*. It's about what's enough for *you*. Once you figure that out, you can wake up and choose your own life. Otherwise, you may end up drifting along in someone else's scarcity story. A story that's not *yours* can't be the source of *your* true happiness, or provide a path to a just and sustainable planet.

> Enough is not about dictating amounts or a particular lifestyle. It is a point of view, a context for the way we orient to ourselves, to one another, organizations, and life itself.

The actions we choose to take will look different for each of us. For some of us this means getting rid of our clutter, giving away old clothes, downsizing our homes, emptying our storage units, and simplifying our lives.

The Sounds of Scarcity

Let's put our thoughts and fears on loudspeaker for a moment. Stop and really listen to the clamor in your head and all around you. This is what we hear every day, all day: "If only I had more time . . . If I could just have a minute to myself . . . If only I could afford . . . If only I were thinner, smarter, faster, richer . . . then . . . then I'd be ok, feel better, do the things I really want to do . . . THEN, I'd be happy! But I'm so tired. *I need more* sleep. More exercise. A better body. Plastic surgery. A nicer, sexier, richer mate. More closet space. New clothes. New phone. New car."

Or maybe the flip side:

"*I have too much* to do. I am drowning. My house is a mess with clutter. I am so overwhelmed. I will never get it all done in time. If I only had one more day in the week or twenty-six hours in a day, then. . . ."

On and on the story goes. We want more time, more space, more sex, more money, *always* more money. No matter how much we have, there is never ever enough money.

Sound familiar?

Ever hear of the allegory about two fish friends swimming in the ocean? A third fish swims by, greets the friends, and says, "Nice water today." After a few moments one fish turns to his friend and says, "Water? What's water?"

> "You are swimming in a sea of scarcity and you don't even know it."
>
> **—Les Traband**

This is our human situation. The water we swim in can be hard to notice. But once we do see it, we have the opportunity to choose something else. That is what happened to us. When we saw the scarcity, its pervasiveness and tenacity, we knew we wanted something different. We hope you will too.

We're stuck in the cycle of consumption. They get rich. You get tired. Their stock price goes up. Your energy drops. They own your mind. You own lots of stuff. You might periodically get the urge to sell it or put it in bags for Goodwill. Or, like so many others, you might keep accumulating and hoarding, letting it fill your houses to the point where nothing more fits. Now you must acquire more space and put stuff in storage because you can't imagine letting it go. You can't afford the stuff or the storage fees. You find yourself in debt, struggling and suffering, caught by an inability to let go, slow down, and stop.

But wait, there's more! Being a workaholic is now considered a badge of honor. We brag about how hard we work (at work, at the gym, as a parent . . .) to prove we are all right.

Whew. Exhausting.

We are playing a game of unlimited consumption that we can't win. We think we can win by outspending, outworking, and out-traveling "the Joneses." After all of our effort and striving, we still feel something is missing. Success, and its constant companion, the quest for more, leaves us tired and afraid.

Annie Leonard, creator of the film *The Story of Stuff*, speaks to our "more is better" lifestyle. She says, "[It] is not even making us happy along the way. It would be one thing if we were having a great time plundering our natural habitat and endlessly consuming. But we are the least happy, most overfed, and undernourished people in history."[1]

Three Levels of Scarcity

In our work we've found three levels of scarcity:

- **Personal scarcity.** *I* am not enough. *I* am not smart enough, sexy enough, wise enough, fast enough, skinny enough, accomplished enough. You get the picture.
- **Interpersonal scarcity.** *You* are not enough. And, "*If* you would just, [fill in the blank here with either

something you want that person to start doing or stop doing], *then* it or you would be ok." This kind of scarcity is pervasive in intimate relationships and in our workplaces. "If *they* had been faster, smarter, more efficient, then *we* would not be in this pickle."

- **Structural scarcity.** This scarcity is built into the system so that for some people, there is really and truly not enough.

All three of these levels of scarcity are operating at the same time. Those of us who have enough to fulfill our needs and some of our wants may live in constant fear that we could lose it all. So, we hold on tight to what we have, and focus on accumulating more so we are never in the position of those who do not have enough to pay the bills.

How We Got Here

A BIT OF BIOLOGY

Our brains have evolved, in part, to search for danger. To do this successfully we instinctively sort for what is different, unusual, or not within the norm. As hunter-gatherers, danger took the shape of a tiger chasing us or another tribe at war with us. We had to constantly search for food and water resources, sometimes requiring a tribe or community to pack up and move elsewhere.

Today, those "tigers" can look like our bosses at work, our competitors who have more resources than we do, and people trying to get ahead of us literally or figuratively.

Beyond that thrust for survival is something else built into us: the capacity to dream, to long, to feel awe, to desire. We seek to reach, to go beyond where we are currently. Following these desires helps us identify, understand, locate, and own our power. By using our power effectively, we help take the scare out of scarcity.

HUMAN HISTORY AND THE BIRTH OF SEPARATION

Human beings were initially nomadic and some still are. Hunting and gathering was the chief method for sustaining human life. We did not store much, if any, food for long periods.

Around ten thousand years ago, many human beings started to cultivate crops. This enabled us to stay in one place, settle and own land. With ownership came the need to defend the land and crops against those who might wish to take them. With agriculture came monarchies, with royalty came cities, and with cities and revolutions came centralized government. It was a steady march to the sea of scarcity from there.

SEPARATING OURSELVES

As our physical biology changed, as well as the social structure of society, we began to see human life as separate from and dominant over all other life. We separated ourselves from nature. We separated mind from body, thinking from feeling. David Loy, a Buddhist teacher, says it well, "The delusive sense of a separate self inside will always be experienced as ungrounded and therefore insecure, so there is also going to be this sense that something is missing. I think that helps explain our obsession with things like money, fame, appearance, and so forth. Thanks to this gnawing sense of lack, we never feel rich enough, famous enough, or beautiful enough."[2]

> What choices would we make—and how would we conduct ourselves—if we knew we were all connected? If we remembered our actions matter, our lives matter, and our conduct affects all of life?

This "myth of separation" is costing us in ways that are staggering to our health, our well-being, our planet, and each other. War, human trafficking, genocide. Pollution, global warming, mass species extinction, all arise from a belief that we are separate and "better than."

THE SIREN SONG OF CONSUMPTION

Have you noticed how often people are referred to as "consumers"? We constantly hear references to consumer confidence, consumer spending, consumer trends, consumer price indexes, and consumer habits.

John Monczunski writes in *Notre Dame Magazine,* "Consuming has become our identity, and if we don't do it at the appropriate time, to the appropriate (excessive) degree, something must be wrong."[3]

Our consumption-based society started with the Industrial Revolution and its legacy of production for the sake of profit. Excess manufacturing capacity after World War II and abundant natural resources made things more readily available. By the 1950s people were consuming more than they had done in Earth's entire history.

Industry in a capitalistic economy invented the consumption cycle: extraction, production, distribution, consumption, and disposal. With planned obsolescence, businesses created disposable goods and then manufactured desire for the latest and greatest of everything.

We have witnessed the dramatic rise of brand names, and "logo branded" merchandise with the logo being the selling point. Now we associate our belonging to a class or tribe with the products we buy. We are literally buying our belonging and social status.

We fuel our consumption and unchecked growth with money we don't have to buy things we probably don't need.

THE SYSTEM IN ACTION

Let's talk about diamonds. In the 1930s, less than 10 percent of women received a diamond engagement ring. Today about 80 percent of women receive a diamond.[4] During the past eighty years, the diamond industry manufactured a story of value, scarcity, and status. They've convinced us that buying a diamond ring is an essential step toward a life of true happiness. But the message is much more insidious: the bigger the diamond, the bigger your love. If your friend's diamond engagement ring is bigger, that surely means their fiancé loves them more than yours does. This is the weapon of comparison. Its goal is to drive you to buy something you don't need, something that won't make you happy, and put you in debt for no good reason.

Scarcity is also woven into how money is created and distributed. In the 2009 documentary *The Money Fix*, Belgian economist Bernard Lietaer discusses how scarcity lives in our banking system. Every dollar in our system is actually debt. Money is created when someone incurs a debt and uses the banks to finance that debt. The money is kept scarce by charging interest on it. There is *always* less money than is needed in the system to pay back the debt. We have created an inherent deficiency in the money supply.

Myths of Scarcity and Excess

Our fear of scarcity is so ingrained we start to believe "this is just the way it is." In *The Soul of Money: Transforming Your Relationship with Money and Life,* Lynne Twist writes, "It's not you and me. It's you or me, and if I have more access to resources and money and labor, I win and you lose." Twist calls this thinking a "myth" because of the power these assumptions have over us.[5]

LYNNE TWIST'S THREE TOXIC MYTHS OF SCARCITY
- There is not enough.
- More is better.
- That's just the way it is.

THREE MYTHS OF EXCESS
In the scarcity story, we believe more of everything will cure what ails us. This comes from three additional myths we call "the myths of excess":

- You can have it all (people make a pretense of it).

- Having it all will make you happy (Instagram lets us edit our lives and only show the good parts—real life can't compete).
- If you do not have it all or you aren't happy, then it's your fault.

These myths keep us in a cycle of consumption and confusion. Even those of us who are aware of the problem continue to struggle to get out from underneath the power of the myths. And while consuming is not wrong, we are grossly out of balance with the other activities of being human.

THE LIES WE TELL OURSELVES

Have you ever heard yourself say, out loud or in your head: "When I lose those last five, ten, twenty-five pounds, then I will feel good"? "Once we buy the house, then...."? "Once I get a new job, then...."?

We often think that a specific change will be the thing that pushes us over the edge into happiness! We believe happiness is just a matter of "more." More money, things, experiences, relationships.

Yet, has this been true for you? Have you lost the weight, gotten the fancier job, gotten the "perfect" relationship and then found yourself in a lasting state of greater joy and sustainable peace?

Be careful here in answering this because many of us have become confused. We are talking about real abiding happiness and joy, not momentary pleasure or satisfaction (which, by the way, we aren't knocking). As author Oliver Burkeman cites, "What's promised by positive thinking and conventional self-help, which seems aimed more at an unbroken state of excitement" is a fallacy.[6]

Advertisers *promise* that our Subaru will connect us to love, or our experiences at Zappos will deliver happiness. We hope and pray that if we spin our thoughts in a particular direction—control their flow and tone and content—we will arrive at a steady, optimal, happy state. In the myths of excess we believe that more things will make us happy. The truth is, once our basic needs are met and we have some extra for fun and security, most research says the further accumulation of stuff not only does not make us happy, it can have the opposite effect.

IT'S NOT YOUR FAULT

There is a false belief that we are all born on the same starting line and have an equal chance of winning the money game. If you miss out, so the thinking goes, you must be lazy, stupid, or both. Yet that's often not true. Companies downsize, jobs move or disappear. There are actual issues of racism, sexism, and other forms of discrimination that can work against you.

We get depressed, addicted, hopeless, and angry. No matter our "intentions" and even our hard work, we can't guarantee success and wealth. You can do all the "right" things and still not get the results you want every time or in the time you thought you would. That's life.

But living and working from a scarcity mind-set doesn't work in the long term, and isn't necessary. You don't need to have it all—you need to find what makes you happy (easier said than done, but worth the effort).

In *The Soul of Money,* Twist recounts a story of meeting and listening to the renowned futurist and thinker Buckminster Fuller who predicted that the world would be making a shift from what he termed a "you *or* me" mind-set to a mind-set of "you *and* me."[7] That Fuller's predictions are starting to come true is evidenced by today's "sharing economy." We each don't have to *own* everything—we can share with others. Think of Lyft and Uber, Zipcar and car2go: they all let you share someone else's car. Airbnb, Couchsurfing, VRBO, and more: they let you share someone else's home.

Those car- and house-sharing models are the very definition of "you *and* me." We both win: the "consumers" win by getting what we need without having to make big investments. The "providers" win in getting help to pay for what they own. The sharing economy helps us see that there is enough, that more is not better, and "just the way it is," is old thinking.

THE WEAPONS OF SCARCITY

There are weapons being deployed to keep us under control. We call these the "weapons of scarcity." They play us, even when we think we're smart enough not to fall for them. Yet even the smartest of us fall into these traps. We've alphabetized this list—but shame and fear tend to be the biggest weapons. Then each of us falls victim to a different weapon of choice depending on the circumstance.

Alienation
Comparison
Competition
Contraction

Discord
Distraction
Doubt
Either/Or
Failure
Fear
Hoarding
Hostility
Immediate and short term
Impatience
Jealousy
Resentment
Resistance
Self-loathing
Shame
Silence
Uncertainty
What isn't
Worry

Each of us may find that one weapon is more often deployed against us—or even *by* us. We may notice that a few are operating at all times and have become personal weapons of mass destruction.

Resentment, for example, is a pervasive weapon of scarcity and we use it against others and ourselves. Once we get a sense of which weapons we most often employ we can begin to catch ourselves starting to wander into scarcity territory.

Comparison can be a potent weapon. We can struggle, always wondering if we measure up to expectations of parents, siblings, teachers, mentors, or colleagues. A friend of ours shared how the comparison weapon led her to a pair of earrings and an aha moment:

> I knew two women who traveled a lot on foreign vacations. They would go to Europe, the Caribbean, or Asia at least once a year, and sometimes twice. I so envied their ability to go on these trips, while I was home childrearing and working to feed my family. One year, they traveled to Hong Kong, and each returned with beautiful sapphire and diamond earrings. They took my breath away. I knew right then that I would be happy and all would be well if I had earrings like that. I expressed my delight with the jewelry, and they even encouraged me to buy a pair because they were so happy with their earrings.
>
> I pestered my husband to buy me said earrings for Christmas that year. We went shopping for them together. When we walked into the jewelry store, I was thrilled. We asked to see earrings *just like* the ones that my friend had bought. Out they came on the tray and my heart sank. They were way beyond what we could afford. However, by then I was hooked and knew that *any* sapphire earrings would make me happy. I had to have some. We picked out a tiny pair of stud earrings and brought them home. When I wore them, I discovered that they did not indeed make me happy. In fact, they made me feel ridiculous.
>
> I've kept those earrings in my jewelry box for thirty years. Whenever I see someone who has an expensive sparkly possession that creates a deep twinge of envy in me, I do two things: I compliment them on their beautiful possession; and I take out my sapphire stud earrings and remember that feeling of emptiness after I bought them. I am not against sparkly expensive things—however, I have learned the lesson that happiness is never born out of a feeling of envy of not having.

So not only do we deploy these weapons toward ourselves and in our relationships, the marketing machine of our economy uses them as fuel to support our overconsumption and distorted relationship to true happiness.

ARE YOU STUCK IN THE SCARCITY STORY?

One way to see this is to return to how we opened this chapter, to recall your first thoughts from this morning. Were they something like, "I didn't get enough sleep," or "I don't have enough time to . . . ."? Did you grab your mobile phone to get started on work before your feet hit the floor?

Now reread the myths: You can have it all, having it all will make you happy, and if you do not have it all or you are not happy, it's your fault.

As you read through these cultural assumptions that we live with as if they were real, start noticing your thoughts, body sensations, and emotions.

> Just noticing how we react to scarcity stories can shift our relationship with them.

If we can make it a practice to become aware of these myths at play in our own life and the lives of others, then we can start to unwind from the toxicity of living a life in scarcity. We invite you to drop your scarcity story and join us.

Practice. Practice. Practice.

The key to unwinding from scarcity is realizing that life is a learning journey. We learn through practice, and we have choices about what and how we practice.

STRUCTURE SHAPES BEHAVIOR

When we practice, we get good at whatever it is we are practicing. This means we even get good at things we are doing unwittingly, or things that no longer serve us.

There are three elements to breaking old habits and crafting new ones:

- Awareness
- Unwinding
- Capacity building

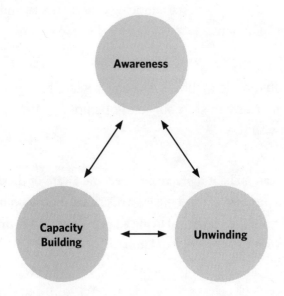

With **awareness** we begin by tracking the sensations we feel and the thoughts and images that arise in our day-to-day lives. We don't need to add to the experience; we can just witness and acknowledge what is happening. This gives us the ability to move through the world by choice rather than reaction and recrimination. We use both self-reflections and inquiry to increase awareness.

Typically, for **unwinding** to happen, we must interrupt our normal behaviors and habits and do something different and then watch and listen. We can engage with a safe person to help guide us. Sometimes we can do it on our own, but it requires safety and an opening to let what needs healing to come forward.

For **capacity building**, we deliberately repeat an action with commitment to strengthen what is there or fill in what is missing. Capacity building takes time. Dabbling with a practice once or twice will very likely not yield much for you. Patience, time, and repetition are required to produce lasting results.

These three elements combined support and interact with each other so we can develop new declarations, write new stories, and take new actions. Let us practice intentionally. Together.

practices to help take the scare out of scarcity

Practice #1:
Am I in Scarcity?

This practice was given to us by a colleague, who put an empty candy dish on his desk at work, and, whenever he was having a scarcity thought, put a penny in the dish. He gave the money away at the end of the month. He was amazed at how many scarcity thoughts he had every day.

We can expand his experiment. You can have a dish at home and at work or carry an empty coin pouch with you and put a scarcity coin in as you travel out in the world. You could put a different coin in depending on your level of scarcity. Deep fear, perhaps a quarter, mild resistance, a penny. Take the money at the end of each month or quarter and gift it to a person or organization creating a world where everyone matters.

Practice #2:
Exploring Scarcity's Biggest Pain Points: Money, Time, and Relationships

Here are a series of practices to help you unwind from these pain points. Write your responses in your journal or notebook.

MONEY

- What is my relationship with money?
- Who taught me about money and what did I learn?
- What does money mean to me? What is money? Where did it come from?
- What does money have to do with time?
- Where am I in scarcity about money? When did I first start to suffer in relationship to money and notice I had too little or too much?
- How do I want to relate to money *now*? Friend, enemy, sibling, lover?
- What secret about money am I willing to admit to myself, and to one other person?
- Am I willing to stop letting the amount of money I have or don't have define me?
- What story am I telling myself about money that is disempowering me? Am I willing to surrender this story?

TIME

- When did I become aware of time? How old was I?
- Who told me about time?
- Who do I know who "manages time" well?
- What are my strategies to manage time? What are my pain points?
- Where in my life does time speed up for me? Where does it slow down?
- What is my natural rhythm? When is my natural rhythm to work, to sleep, to clean, to make love?

- When did I notice giving up on that rhythm to fit into something?
- How have I adjusted to others' rhythms to stay connected or belong and what has the impact been?
- How is my relationship to time right now?
- What stories do I tell myself about time? (e.g., I don't have enough. I need five more hours in a day. I need another day in the week. If only I had more time, then [fill in the blank].)
- If I look through the lens of the weapons of scarcity and connect them to time, what do I see? (e.g., obligation, comparison, what is not, discord, worry, impatience, contraction, immediate and short-term, resistance, either/or.)
- How would my life be if I knew I had all the time in the world? If I knew I actually had power in relationship to time? If I knew you could play with time?

RELATIONSHIPS

- Using a piece of paper, mark yourself the middle and write the names of the people who are in your life and put them at the distance they feel from you. Do this your way, with your chosen writing utensil. Don't overthink it, just sketch out: Who is in your life, and where do you place them? When you are complete, look at your relationship map and inquire:
- Who is in my life? Who is missing?
- What kinds of relationships do I have? Friends, colleagues, lover(s), children, extended family, family of origin, neighbors, etc. How do I categorize or label those in my life?

- Where did I place them and why? What narratives do I have about the people in my life?
- Now that you have mapped out your relationships you may have noticed people whom you are "closer" to and "further" from. Notice how these distances are working for, or against you.
- Appreciate what's working. Consider how you can change what isn't.

law 1
stories
matter

What is my story?

We begin our journey by recognizing the stories we tell ourselves, and the ones handed to us as a birthright. These stories become a set of invisible forces—social, cultural, economic, and environmental—that are shaping our beliefs and assumptions. They can have undue influence on our behavior and the narrative of our life.

Yet we have the power to create and write our own story.

In the movie *The Truman Show,* the protagonist, Truman Burbank, played by Jim Carrey, thinks he has chosen a life for himself. Life is almost perfect—certainly sufficient. He believes it is all of his own making, that he wrote his own story and is living it. What becomes apparent as the movie progresses is that he is the star of a reality TV show. Everything in his environment has been carefully scripted. He thinks he's in control, but he didn't write his own story. Instead, it was commissioned by a corporation, and he's just a pawn for their profit.

Maybe our own personal "show" isn't so different. We awaken each morning, get dressed, and begin our work. It's easy to be oblivious to the forces shaping our lives.

There's a famous cartoon that we like to use to illustrate this point. The cartoon shows a couple talking inside of a snow globe. One partner says to the other: "Yeah, ever since we've moved in we've been frequented by sudden earthquakes followed by massive snowstorms."

The couple in the snow globe have no idea that they're inside a world that's generating their experience. It's like gravity: we don't have to understand it, believe in it, or even know it's there for it to keep us tethered to the earth.

The same is true with story; it is simultaneously invisible and all around us, like air, shaping our existence.

Our Stories Matter

We are made of stories. It's part of the magic of being human. In the documentary *Planetary*, Brian Swimme tells us, "The *story* is the most essential organizing power within the human experience."[8]

We are woven together in the fabric of creation by layers of stories. Story is the structure that reveals our feelings, thoughts, and behaviors. Our beliefs about the world and all its inhabitants are woven into our stories about life, which, in turn, help define our beliefs. And so, they go round and round, each reinforcing the other.

Since we were born, we have been hearing stories and living with the echo of stories told by others long gone. Every culture has creation stories: stories about why we are here and how we got here in the first place. We tell stories about the species and who we are in relation to the rest of life and the planet itself. We tell stories about each other, about land, about truth and justice. We tell stories about the past and the future. We allow others to tell stories for us and about us.

These layers of story shape everything. We are Truman Burbank, living in a world of stories told to us, then recited by us. The stories are so strong that we often fail to examine and reflect on the impact they have on our lives.

When we look carefully, we see that we reside in multiple stories at once, all pressing on us and shaping us like clay. We're living inside the socioeconomic story of growth and success. We were born into the story of our family—its history, relationships, religion, and beliefs. And finally, we have our personal story— you, your life. Story surrounds us, holding us, cradling us, and sometimes imprisoning us.

Stuck Inside Our Stories

In the invisibility of story, we can start to hold our beliefs and views as *right*. These fixed beliefs can become definitive and immutable, our view, the only view, and then they get exalted as "*the truth*." These thoughts change how we see ourselves and behave in the world. They become our life.

We each have stories about our sex, race, religion, relationships. But just because we've been told a story again and again does not make it true—or unchangeable.

Stories hold such a powerful place in the brain that it does not often register anything outside the story line. The brain is designed to look for evidence to support the stories we think are true. This means stories filter our world, shaping the landscape we see and all that we miss.

There is a well-known sociological experiment that illustrates this point perfectly. People are shown a video of two groups passing a basketball. The people viewing the players are asked to count how many times people wearing white shirts pass a basketball during the short video.

With all their attention on the basketballs, over half of the viewers don't notice a person in a gorilla costume walking across the basketball court! They have all of their attention on the story about counting passes. The guy in the gorilla suit is not part of that story and thus remains invisible to most of the people looking.[9]

The technical term for this is "inattentional blindness," when we fail to notice something *unexpected* that is in plain sight. Of course, there are folks who see the gorilla the first time they watch the video. They're not constrained by the story of counting passed basketballs and see something outside the confines of the story given.

When we are free from our stories or can hold them lightly with room to let in new information, we are able to discover and create new stories, new cosmologies, and new futures.

More often though, stories can blind us—even as we strive to name what we want in our lives. Look at our political environment. Conservatives have stories about liberals. Liberals about conservatives. City people have stories about rural people. Folks in the middle of the country have stories about folks who live on the coasts and vice versa.

None of these stories are *completely* true. Yet, when we listen to our favorite news sources, the ones that agree with us, the stories seem true. It's in the "seeming" that it becomes real. This is how everything, from stereotypes to unconscious biases, get solidified in our cultural narratives.

The good news is that people invented those stories and we can create new ones.

To tell stories is human. To choose the story is an act of leadership. We are at a juncture in human history when the stories we have been telling are not working. They are leading to destruction of our planet, inequities, and widespread unhappiness.

We don't have to be the prisoners of the stories that were handed to us. We are not fated to play out only the stories we were born into.

Language Shapes Our Stories

In *The Soul of Money* John Perkins is quoted as saying, "We dreamed it: therefore, it is. I have become convinced that everything we think and feel is merely perception: that our lives—individually as well as communally—are molded around such perception, and that is if we want to change, we must alter our perception. When we give our energy to a different dream, the world is transformed. To create a new world, we must first create a new dream."[10]

We have opportunities to create new dreams all the time. We call it visioning, or creating a business plan, or planning our dream vacation. These dreams—our waking dreams—become our stories. We share dreams through language, making language one of the most powerful tools that we have at our disposal.

Fernando Flores, a Chilean biologist, author, engineer, and entrepreneur, suggests that language is not simply a tool we use to describe a world that already exists, but *rather an action that produces a world and a future that would otherwise not have existed.*[11] In other words, our speaking creates our world.

In the seventeenth century, the rationalist era emerged, the era of objective truth. There is a world out there. We can know it. Our job is to observe things as they are happening and then to describe what we have observed. This is the basis for deductive reasoning. This story has been and remains what fuels scientific thinking. This has been the paradigm in place for five hundred years.

Just like we discovered that it was not *true* that the world was flat, there has been a new conversation introduced by the scientific and philosophical communities. This quantum paradigm is based on the innovations in the field of quantum physics. This new view suggests that we interact with our environment and "cocreate" the reality we see. We cannot observe or measure an experiment without impacting the experiment. Our physical presence alters the outcome.

This is a profound shift in our relationship to the world. It implies we are not describers of an objectively knowable world, fixed and the same for everyone. Rather, we are designers and authors of a world with which we interact. Our speaking actually makes things real and then drives behavior.

Stories as Actions through Language

We'll focus on three speech acts that are critical to the creation of stories: declarations, assessments, and assertions.

DECLARATIONS

Let's look at the power of *declarations*, starting with marriage. Where does marriage exist? Is it out there somewhere? Is it the piece of paper you sign? Can you go and find a marriage anywhere in the physical world? No. Marriage is a declaration made through language and backed up with a certain set of practices we collectively agree constitute being married. There is no physical thing called "marriage" out there. We say, "I do" or "I will." Then an official declares that we are married. And, presto, we are.

It all happened because we said so. We declare and something comes into being that was not there before. You and I have that power too. Every sacred text from every tradition uses declaration to tell their origin story, including Genesis, "And God said, 'Let there be light,' and there was light."

Many of us are living inside of declarations made long ago in a faraway place called our childhood. Some we made, and some were made for us before we were even born. Some of those declarations served us well for a long time. Some might have even saved our lives. Like when we tell ourselves, "I will never feel like that again." Or when we say, "I will survive no matter what they do to me."

These declarations then become guiding principles, often invisible to us, but guiding nonetheless, and we live according to them, faithfully, often until we want something else that we cannot have if we keep living inside the old declarations. Old forgotten declarations that are running our lives will often interfere with our ability to fulfill on declarations we want to make now.

Take, for example, a client who had never been in a lasting relationship. She wanted one. At least she "declared" it so. But lurking further back in her life was an older declaration, one more embedded, one to which she was being more faithful. She told herself she was never going to let anyone hurt her again. She was going to be safe by being alone. And it worked. It got her out of a terrible childhood situation. It got her to be resilient and strong and capable. But it wasn't getting her a lasting love relationship. To love, we have to open up and be vulnerable, which opens us to being hurt. In her case, it might mean violating a secret oath she took to never get hurt again.

Sometimes declarations get made for us. "No daughter of *mine* will talk that way or act that way." "No son of *mine* will be like that." "You will go to a *good* school." "We are not like *those* people." It goes on and on.

These declarations are the seeds that take root and turn into full-blown stories about ourselves, life, people, and the world. Before declarations grow into stories they have the power to set direction, open up new possibilities, and help us set a course toward something. To declare is to design. To declare is to create. To declare is to steer.

Then we use assessments and assertions to turn declarations into full-blown stories that we believe are *the* truth.

ASSESSMENTS

The word "assessment" is defined as "the evaluation or estimation of the nature, quality, or ability of someone or something." In other words, it's a fancy way of saying "opinion."

Here's an example: "She is smart." We may think of a statement like this as true or false. But let's slow down. Is it? Who defines smart? What is smart? *Our* smart may be *your* stupid. In this case, it's made because we have a shared story of what it means to be smart.

But here is the kicker. Just because we share a story widely and *believe it* doesn't make it a fact. It just makes it a shared story—a belief. Our collective agreement about the story is what gives it power.

Money is one of the best examples of this. What is money? Paper? Yes. What about numbers on a spreadsheet? Or the number in your bank account? An agreement? Truth? Money is a complex set of agreements with far-reaching power, possibly more power than any other agreement.

An assessment can be grounded or ungrounded. Grounding means that you have a basis for judging that your judgment is useful, based on 1) a history of past action, 2) specified standards, or 3) there not being opposing assessments that are as well grounded. We say money is a grounded assessment.

We are constantly churning out assessments about ourselves and others as if they were fact. That's dangerous, because our assessments lead to our assertions. Unless we're clear about whether something is an assessment or a fact, our assertions, decisions, and actions can be flawed.

ASSERTIONS

Assertions are defined as "a confident and forceful statement of fact or belief." Fact and belief are two different things. Fact is generally accepted as true—like gravity. We feel and see its effects all around us.

But assertions don't have to be facts. When you say, "The sky is blue," is that a fact, or an assertion? Well, if we know something about color and the eye and refracted light, then the sky being blue is not so clearly true or false. It's a matter of the observer seeing through a certain lens. Is the sky *always* blue? If you are color blind, is the sky *ever* blue?

There are people who assert that global warming is a hoax. Their assertions are based on beliefs, not facts. Yet, when people make forceful assertions, we can confuse them with facts because they're presented with such authority.

What we accept as fact or fiction might actually be an assessment made by someone with a set of stories they *believe* are true. This applies to our own stories as well.

Being in Charge of Your Own Story

Once we can discern our opinion from what actually happened, we have room to create and write our own stories.

That said, we don't have control over everything that happens. People die. Parents misbehave. Despots take power. It rains on our wedding day. Our children say things we wish they would not. It helps to accept there are many things in life over which we have little or no control.

However, *everything* that happens after the fact is up to us. This is true even when it comes to big stories, like the story of race, or the story of gender. We choose what stories we tell—or retell. Further, we are responsible for the actions we take on their behalf and their consequences.

Can you see yourself in charge of your own storytelling and story making? This is a big responsibility and gives us the power and opportunity to create a life that works, a life we love.

Ruby Sales, civil rights activist and teacher, told the story of her upbringing in an African American community in the segregated south, "I grew up believing that I was a first-class human being and a first-class person. And our parents were spiritual geniuses who were able to shape a counterculture of Black folk religion that raised us from disposability to being essential players in society. And it also taught us something serene about love. I love everybody. I love everybody. I love everybody in my heart. And so, hate was not anything in our vocabulary."[12] This is the power of declaration and story in action.

THE EMBODIED STORY

In *Holding the Center: Sanctuary in a Time of Confusion*, Richard Strozzi-Heckler writes, "Our experiences shape our body, and our body, in turn, shapes our relationship with the world. We are living patterns of organization."[13] Stories become embedded in the collective and then shape the culture itself. Architecture becomes a reflection of the culture's values. Economies become a reflection of our current collective values. All organizations built within a national culture and climate become a reflection of the national mood.

When we begin our leadership trainings at Seven Stones, we say, "*You* are the first organization you must master." As much as we live and construct life through language we must recognize that we move through the world inside the body, our *entire* body. Discovering the embodied story requires a new lens, a post-Cartesian one, where the mind lives in the body, not somehow separate from it. The body is the primary context of the human experience. The brain (not to be confused with the mind) is distributed throughout the body by our central nervous system. Each of us has a unique biology that responds to life in many ways. In the face of threat or distress the nervous system responds by fighting, fleeing, or freezing.

If we repeat this response to distress often enough, we develop a pattern in response to situations that seem similar on some level. We call this "somatic shaping." Like clay, our musculature and neurophysiology actually become molded by life and our responses to it. Life literally shapes us.

Because we are creatures of habit and pattern we begin to relate to life from that habituated set of responses. We experience something. It triggers our physiology. That physiological response can cause a story to flare up that was operating beneath the surface of our conscious awareness.

The story is there already, kind of like a sleeping dragon. Then something happens that triggers the story and off we go.

In a culture that prizes mind over body, we often don't even notice when we have an emotional and physiological response. We go right to story. That said, if we slow down enough we can see that story is an embodied phenomenon.

As Bruce Lee so aptly put it, "Under duress we do not rise to our own expectations, we fall to the level of our training." The story from the past can trigger a habituated nervous system response. A nervous system response can trigger an old story lodged literally into the tissues, into the neurophysiological history of that person.

We practice stories embedded within us from long ago without knowing we are doing it. Then we wonder why we cannot seem to get to our desired future state. Once trained into us, unless we apply conscious attention and intentions, our habits will override our desires every time.

Story alone will not get us where we are going. We must reweave the body, mind, and spirit back into wholeness. Then we get to reweave ourselves back into the fabric of nature one stitch at a time.

CREATING A NEW STORY

Let's recap:

- Language has power.
- We have the ability to see the existing story for what it is.
- Then we can discern the forces at work in creating the layers of stories that make up our lives.

- We have opportunities to create new stories for ourselves. We can go on to dream bold new futures and declare our intentions based on what we care most about.
- Story is embodied. It's why we introduced practice and the idea that practice matters right away.
- Without practices the ideas presented here, like so many, become what one of our colleagues calls, "shelf help." We read. We get inspired. We attempt. We fail. We become resigned. We think it's our fault. Out of our longing however we try again. When we see that our stories are not fully of our own making, and we recognize that practice is critical to our success, we have a real chance for something radically new to happen. With this extraordinary power to create through language and practice comes a kind of humbling responsibility. Given this power, what will you create today?

WE ARE NOT ALONE

We are not creating alone. We are interacting with all kinds of other forces, some visible, some invisible, which are impacting us in ways we mostly do not understand to support our declarations. When we blend the power of language with an acknowledgment of the unseen causes and conditions, we can be open to the outcome manifesting in surprising ways, and in forms we did not quite imagine.

Accepting the invisible invites us to be soft and receptive to new information as we travel the road to manifestation. Some people report feeling a sense of humility because we are, in a way, surrendering to something larger than just us.

Some people call this co-creation and many see it as an accurate representation of what is actually happening. For some of us this is our relationship with God, Jesus, higher power, nature, spirit. Regardless of the names we use or the names we do not use, we're speaking of a larger intelligence here—the energy that made this universe.

This stance allows us to blend or join with the rhythms around us. We practice harmony and flow with forces outside of our control, not resisting or going slack to them, but being with them.

We are joining our intention, our attention, our hearts and minds with something unseen and powerful in the hopes that, together, we might bring to reality that which lives in our dreams.

INTUITION

We can readily access our intuition by creating a partnership with those mysterious forces and the people and circumstances that arise. Intuition involves those voices we hear when we are quiet and listening. For some of us, that might be prayer, meditation, or a walk in the woods. The advice we hear can be incredible.

What is available to us when we are listening in this co-creative, receptive space? This type of manifestation requires us to direct our attention to our new dream in order for it to become realized.

It's not just magic, it's science. Energy follows attention and then becomes form as it gets more and more concentrated.

BLESSING PRACTICE

With consistent intention engaged in a cocreative process, we can indeed receive that which we desire, including a life of enough. As opposed to "I will" or "I am," we work with "May I" or "May you" or "May this . . . ."

The essence of using a blessing practice of "may I/we/you/this" has an entirely different quality than the action of declaration. We could say the action of a blessing has a yin, or receptive, cocreative quality, and declaration has a yang, or assertive, directive quality.

We invoke the mysterious forces of senses beyond the scientifically proven five senses and allow for higher intelligence to flow toward manifestation. Both of these qualities are of enormous value when we are in the world trying to get things done. We need both at different moments and we must practice both to discover for ourselves when they are each most potent and effective. Blessings, declarations, assertions, and assessments become the building blocks of the story of enough. And our story of enough can become the life we live.

practices
for law 1

Practice #1:

A Daily Inventory Self-Inquiry

This practice can help throughout the day and allows us to pause and see
what stories we are telling ourselves. You can set an alarm on your phone
or complete the process at each meal break, pick the timing that feels
comfortable. You may choose to write answers in a notebook or draw in a
journal. Feel free to reflect on all the questions or just choose one or two;
make this work for your needs.

UPON WAKING

- How am I?
- Who or what is nourishing me?
- What do I need to write down to clear my mind?
- What intention will I create today?
- What conversations call to me today?
- What actions require my attention?
- What foods nourish me?
- What foods don't work for me?
- Who can I tell I love?
- What needs completing?
- Where can I invest my time, money, or talents today?

- Where can I help?
- What is enough today?

NOON

- What can I acknowledge and appreciate myself for in this moment?
- Is my breath flowing throughout my body?
- Are there urgent matters that require my attention?
- Are there things I planned to do that aren't as relevant as I thought?
- Is the intention I set this morning present for me?

EVENING

- What am I grateful for?
- Where did scarcity grip me?
- Where did I feel connected today?
- What do I need to do, say, or write to be complete for this day?

Practice #2:
I AM... the Beginning of My Story.

Joseph Goldstein and Jack Kornfield relate a famous, and significant, story in their book *Seeking the Heart of Wisdom: The Path of Insight Meditation*.

It is said that soon after his enlightenment, the Buddha passed a man on the road who was struck by the extraordinary radiance and peacefulness of his presence. The man stopped and asked, "My friend, what are you? Are you a celestial being or a god?"

"No," said the Buddha.

"Well then, are you some kind of magician or wizard?"

Again, the Buddha answered, "No."

"Are you a man?"

"No."

"Well, my friend, what then are you?"

The Buddha replied, "I am awake."[14]

Every declaration of self begins with I AM and starts our story. I AM is the first declaration every human makes. It is the opening of our very first story. As we develop we keep declaring, consciously or unconsciously. Try it now.

I AM.

I AM HERE.

I AM ENOUGH.

I AM_____.

What new story are you willing to create?

Practice #3:
Assess Your Declarations: An Inventory

This practice is great to do now as you are diving into the ideas in this book and then again on a monthly basis. You may choose to do this practice alone or with a learning buddy or intimate partner.

Consider how you speak and the declarations you make. What effect have they had on your life and work?

- What declarations have you made that have become the story of who you are?
- What practices do you have that allow you to live in the story of your choosing? For example, daily writing, movement practice, regular prayer or meditation practice.
- What declarations have you made that no longer serve you yet still run your life? This is a way to look at what is old, in the background, or in conflict with our current declarations.
- What is the biggest declaration you have ever made? For example, wedding vows, or committing to raise a child.
- What declaration is lurking in the background that you know needs to be made, and that will alter everything? Perhaps relationships that need to end, a new career, or returning to your childhood home.
- What declaration, if made, would catalyze a huge breakthrough in your team, in your organization, in your life?

Practice #4:
My Emotional Autobiography

This practice is adapted from the work of the Strozzi Institute.

This is an opportunity to write your emotional autobiography. We recommend that after you write your story you share it. Maybe to a group of like-hearted friends committed to living within the seven laws. There are many reasons to write and share your story:

- The things we share we can heal.
- Telling your story creates intimacy and builds community.
- Telling your story gives you the opportunity to reinterpret the past and invent a new future.
- Telling your story breaks isolation.

Here are some basic guidelines for writing your EA: First, write the autobiography as your present self. It can be as short or long as you like. Most people write eight to fifteen pages. You may write in chronological order or you may group events into categories. Make sure that this is not simply a report of events. Avoid long descriptions, but rather focus on how you were shaped and impacted by the events that took place.

Some questions to orient you:

- What stories and traditions did you grow up with? How did their prevailing attitudes and beliefs affect you?
- How did the historical context in which you were raised impact your view of yourself, your possibilities, and your future?
- How were you shaped by the events that took place in your life?
- How has your history helped or hindered your ability to see possibilities about your life and your future?

- How were you shaped by important people in your life?
- How have traumatic events shaped your emotional autobiography?
- What stories, beliefs, and injunctions were you born into that no longer serve you, but you are still using?
- If you could change part of the past what part would you change?
- What stops you from making change—how is change understood by your family and history?

Practice #5:
Creating the Future from the Future

Creating our story for the future is a powerful declaration practice that can be done at any time. We often create at the beginning of the year, month, or quarter. We have heard others call this exercise "Back to the Future" or a "Merlin Process."

For this exercise, *imagine* it is the end of the year (event, meeting, class) and you are sitting with a dear friend, your spouse, or coach and relaying to them how the intervening time was spent.

Talk as if the time has passed in your year or event. Report on what happened, what worked and what didn't. Note how you spent your time; what brought you joy and all that you accomplished. Note who and what you are grateful for. Take time to write this in your journal or type it up in your personal notes.

Put it away for at least twenty-four hours. When you return, reread what you wrote. What do you notice? Are there any tweaks to make?

Given what you wrote, make a list of actions you must take to fulfill on this future. Enroll a friend to be your accountability partner to help you stay on track while you live into your future.

law 2
i am
enough

What is happening now? How is that enough?

"I am enough." That simple declaration allows us to place ourselves at the center of our lives. This law is critical—it helps us create a bridge from the scarcity story to a new story, the *story of enough.* Inside *enough* we can move to the present and live in the now.

Right now, as we are, with whatever we have, whatever we do, whatever mood we are in. In this present moment, we have the power to declare:

- "I am enough."
- "I do enough."
- "I have enough."

Once we make this courageous move, we can author a new story that allows for us to belong, rest, and love. This is our moment, a moment to rewrite our story, to begin again. Yes, you are enough! To even say it means that somewhere out there is a question that needs answering. Are you? Am I? Do I really have enough? Am I truly enough? Who gets to say anyway? In the very asking of the question we may begin to feel like something is wrong. Not wrong with the question, but with us.

What if questions like, "Am I smart enough or pretty enough or tall enough or thin enough or accomplished enough?" were off the table? Can you begin to imagine it? A world in which we did not ask because the questions themselves pointed to something so absurd we could not even fathom it. What if every human already knew they were incredible, gifted, acceptable just as they were and not riddled with doubts about their own worthiness, well-being, and sense of deserving?

Say this to yourself, *"I am enough right now, just as I am, whole and complete."* It's time to take the debate off the table and assume it to be so. When we awaken from the mind-numbing, addictive, alienating illusion of scarcity and excess, we find the truth of our *enoughness.*

A Trigger Warning

This can be the beginning of something great—a new view of the world from which to create a life we always wanted. That said, it's important for to us to issue one gentle but critical warning: as one of our mentors warned us, once you declare *enough*, scarcity will come and find you. It will seek you out, asking you to feed it again, love it again.

When our business was young we regularly found ourselves in the midst of a cash flow crunch. Scarcity gripped Jen. If we did not get paid, what would happen? She could not afford to not be paid. She had some buffer but not a lot and bills were due.

The scarcity voice was loud and crazy and Jen told Gina all of her thoughts of impending doom. Gina, keeping a cool head, suggested an experiment. She told Jen to go and look at what was in the business bank account. This did nothing to relax Jen. And we do mean nothing.

Ok, now what? Gina told Jen to then write a check for 10 percent of what was left in the account. "What? Are you totally crazy? Have you heard nothing I have been saying about our impending doom and lack of resources and the fact that I have a husband who has been sick and is still rebuilding his business and on and on . . . ."

Trying to contain herself, Jen asked Gina what she was supposed to do with said check. Gina said, "Pick someone or something to give it too."

Jen was flabbergasted. Seriously? Take what little we have left and give it away? Then Jen thought about the food pantry she saw that day when driving her daughter to school. She saw people,

people who looked like her, lined up waiting to get help from the pantry.

She wrote the check, literally shaking as she signed her name. Later that morning, Jen drove into the pantry parking lot, got out, and walked in. She handed the staff member who worked there the check and headed off to see a client . . . something shifted.

Let us unpack this one for a moment. It was true that we had little in the account. It was true that it meant that Jen was likely not going to get paid on time. It is also true that the level at which she was terrified was totally out of proportion with reality. We had money owed to us. We had enough to get by that week and the week after. We had friends with more money than us and could (even though Jen wasn't one to ask) have asked for help. We even had a local pantry that could and would support us if it came to that.

Jen had never in her life actually been without a meal. The terror she was experiencing was a result of our societal training to always be afraid that there will not be enough. This is the kind of distortion that happens when we are steeped in a culture of fear. We are operating within a complex intersection of dynamics and Gina invited Jen to break the spell of scarcity with a simple but radical practice.

It worked. Jen did not die. She gave something away when it looked and seemed as if there was not enough for her. Strange, right? The money came in. She was ok. Still scared, but less so, because the truth of life is always, and we do mean always, better than the delusion of separation and fear. The depth of our fear in relationship to the culture of scarcity is not to be underestimated. No matter where we fall in the pecking order, the culture of scarcity has distorted our minds. It's closed our hearts and pushed us to act in ways fundamentally out of alignment with the best of who we are and the reality of life. Same holds true for the client of ours who is in scarcity because her electricity got turned off to the client who owns a Maserati having panic attacks about money.

Sacred Enough Meditation

Sit in a comfortable position. You can sit in a chair, or you can be cross-legged on the floor. You can even lie on the floor with your knees bent. Just get comfortable. Whatever works for you in this moment is fine. Take a few deep inhalations and exhalations and read the following. Let the words wash over you. Allow yourself to pause and take in this moment and you may notice a small shift in your experience of life.

You were a gift from the gods at the moment of your birth. Let's touch on the moments of your life when you were enough:

The moments when you did not need anything more
than what was already here.
The moments when you did not compete.
The moments when you had no worry.
The moments when suffering disappeared for you.
The moments when you were not afraid.

Notice what comes into view, what sensations arise. What memories emerge?

If nothing from the past arises, sit in the present moment and ask yourself the two simple questions we opened the chapter with. See what becomes available.

What is happening now?

How is that enough?

Our Relationship to Enough

We are enough right now, just as we are, whole and complete.

Our relationship to enough begins with a declaration and ends with a deep embodied and abiding knowing that we are enough. When we declare that we are enough, we can see in bold relief the stories we tell that are anything but the story of our enoughness. We find the bravery to tell the truth of who we are and how our stories have shaped us. This truth will set us free. When we speak our truth, we can begin to let go: let go of a mind-set that no longer serves; let go of the weapons of scarcity that keep us stuck; let go of the myths that have us believe we are not enough.

When we finally relax into knowing we are whole already—our lust, our quest, our forward thrust for more can end. We consider "more" the holy grail of our time. And once seen clearly, kind of like the wizard behind the curtain, it will be revealed for the red herring it is, and our model of reality will crumble right before our very eyes. More will not cure what ails us. Infinite accumulation on a finite plane will not lead to lasting or sustained happiness. When we see clearly through the lies we have been told about life, meaning, happiness, success, and individualism, we can begin to revel in what is already here. What is here is our own exquisite enoughness, a real abundance grounded in what is truly sustainable and sustaining of all life. This invites the best of the human possibility.

Are You Ready for Awakening?

We are born fully complete, creative, resourceful, and capable. Regardless of our background and childhood experiences, our level of education and wealth, or the strength or weakness of our personal relationships, we can all forget that we are enough. That is why enough can feel uncomfortable or even unreal. We would even go so far as to say that our culture, particularly global consumer culture, thrives on us forgetting.

With our forgetting, we overlook the fact that right now there is enough for everyone on earth to thrive. Really and truly thrive. We, the human race, have enough resources to house everyone in humane and sustaining conditions. There is enough wealth to solve most problems we face. There is enough brain trust—enough great ideas and innovative thinking, enough education, enough organizations working to improve what's not working. There is enough social media technology, so powerful that it allows movements to form and overthrow dictators. There is enough food to feed us all several times over. There is still enough clean water, for now. Resources are finite, yet sufficient to care for all beings.

Spaceship Earth

There is a great and profound intelligence built into this natural world. Water knows how to clean itself; ecosystems know how to rebalance when they get off-kilter. Life sustains itself through the process of renewal, cooperation, and evolution. The temperature is within a perfect range to keep us alive and our air contains the exact amount of gases that work with our lungs. Our planet is a living system that provides everything needed to live and grow and thrive: fruit-bearing trees, wood and clay to build homes, plants and herbs to heal wounds, water teeming with fish and oxygen readily available to keep us alive. There is bounty everywhere we look and all of it was given to all beings free of charge, at least originally it was.

Everything that is required for all of life to flourish indefinitely—the plants, the animals, and the biosphere that contains us—was provided to us by Earth's creation itself. No one, not even humans, had to prove anything in particular to get it. No one earned it and no one envisioned it, strategized to get it or own it. Water, earth, air, fire, food, and resources to stay warm and dry were just given, offered to any and all creatures. The Earth was an equal opportunity provider with everyone qualified to receive right from the start. And miraculously the intelligence built in for us to learn to hunt, and find medicinal plants and read constellations and find water. There was no school other than Earth school.

> It's about knowing—through
> experimentation, inquiry, and practice—
> the threshold that gets us to "enough" and
> letting go of the habitual drive for more.

This second law of enough offers us a way of organizing our lives, our work, our social systems, and our economy. This model suggests that we are enough exactly how we are right now. We do enough each day, each week, each year, and we have enough of whatever it is that's required within ourselves, our relationships, and collectively as a society. Our knowing we are enough offers us a way to speak about what is already happening on the planet. There is a growing and emergent movement with roots in the wisdom traditions, sustainability practices, and new economics. This is being forwarded by stewards, like you, who are willing to do the inner work and practices required to change our collective drama.

Enough is a mind-set: it is the way we listen and speak to ourselves and to others in order to discover our true needs and values. Enough guides us to align our actions with clear priorities, thus allowing us to find and create a life of sustainable abundance. This new story we are inviting you to move into is an antidote to the anxiety, fear, distraction, shame, and all the other weapons of scarcity. Enough, once declared, has the power to change our orientation, offering us a set of values to rest within, and empowering us to act in new ways. Shifting consciousness and culture takes effort. Shifting from one set of operating principles to another, when still embedded in a system operating from the old principles, causes friction both within ourselves and in our world. This friction is the impetus for change, but change of this sort can be uncomfortable and, therefore, a challenge.

Where to Begin

Where do we begin? Right here with the declaration, even if you don't feel it or believe it. This is where we start: "I am enough." Period. End of sentence. Paragraph. Page. Chapter. Claiming that we are enough opens up the pathway out of our scarcity story. Enough is a context, a space, a view from which to act, not the action itself, or a definition or a diagnosis or a criterion. It is both a revelation and a declaration. It is a remembering of that which is given by our birth, by our Earth, and a stand in that truth. And once we have had it, once we have tasted it, once we have embodied this knowing, everything changes.

Out of declaration, creation arises, from the Big Bang to Genesis in the Bible, as May Sarton writes, "the moment of creation assures that all is well."[15] Or as we believe, the moment of creation assures that there is enough. We humans were designed with the power to create: to create life itself; create story, which is the framework for all human understanding; create new ideas; create physical structures; create beauty through art, dance, and music. We can take what is already given and create something completely new from what is freely offered, including a new mind-set. Investigating our interior life, our mind-set, thoughts, and emotions offers us a pathway to remember the truth of enough. We say "remember" because that knowing of what is enough is our forgotten truth of life on Earth. Enough does not have to be earned, we see knowing our enoughness as a living phenomenon. In our work with our clients, enough is the framework from which we operate. We stand in the remembrance of our clients' wholeness, completeness, for their already-enoughness. We do not try to fix them or their problems, for they do not require fixing. We offer opportunities for learning, healing, and for development, for their own personal and professional leadership. There is no canned, one-size-fits-all response to our struggles, or to the world's. Rather, we believe that embedding the framework of enoughness into the conversation creates a radical shift in view. The mind-set and evolving story of enough provides people with a new approach to facing problems that leads to solutions that are inclusionary, innovative, nimble, and sustainable over time and can benefit all involved.

WHAT IS YOUR "ENOUGH?"

What's enough for *you*? Like so many simple questions the answers can be complicated. We can't tell you what *your* enough is, but we can help you find it for yourself.

We started on our journeys to enoughness by participating in our Boston Sufficiency Team. This was a learning community where we met and began our journeys toward sustainable abundance.

When Gina first started with the Boston Sufficiency Team, enough actually meant more. *More* clothes for her boys so she could do laundry *less* often. That gave her more time to be with them and less time doing chores. As her boys grew, she also saw that living in a small cottage with four people that also was the headquarters for Seven Stones was simply not *practical*. It *wasn't* enough. She needed a larger house to accommodate her teenage sons *and* growing business. So when *enough* changes, so can you.

We know sometimes a hard-and-fast rule helps. However, we believe that each traveler on this journey has to find their own expression of enough. We do not have the perfect answer. We don't want to impose any one way upon anyone.

And we don't have to, because once we embrace that *we are enough*, our unique expression of life will unfold. If we begin with our own enoughness, we can rest in our sacredness and stop debating its truth. When we can simply *be* enough, we can act from a centered place inside of ourselves.

THE TOOLS OF SUFFICIENCY

We can fight the weapons of scarcity with some of the tools below. They help us let go of the worry, fear, hostility, competition, and our false sense of control. We've listed these in alphabetical order, but different laws speak to different people. Where *shame* and *fear* are the biggest weapons, *love* is the greatest tool.

- Allowing
- And
- Appreciation
- Community
- Creation
- Flow
- Following my heart
- Generosity
- Gratitude
- Harmony
- Humor
- Inquiry
- Listening
- Love
- Nature
- Now
- Nurture
- Oneness
- Openness

- Pause
- Peace
- Truth, transparency, and trust
- What is
- Win-win

As Alan Price wrote in the foreword to *Unstuck: Make the Shift*, "What we have seen is that the *Weapons of Scarcity* must be named and disarmed before the *Tools of Sufficiency* can be deployed with full effectiveness. On the inner journey to peace and greater purpose we must literally turn our mental and emotional swords into ploughshares."

GENEROSITY: EXPERIENCE SUSTAINABLE ABUNDANCE

In the introduction, our first "workout" illustrated how gratitude is a key gateway to enough and the state of sustainable abundance.

Generosity is our second practice to remind ourselves that we are enough in this moment. Generosity can include giving away items you don't need or use, giving someone money or food that you won't miss. Generosity could be a methodical practice of giving a percentage of your salary, growing an extra row of food in your garden, or saying "yes" every time you are asked for money. Fundamentally, the practice of generosity puts us in touch with these truths:

- We are interdependent and not alone.
- We are already relying on the generosity of others to live.
- Our liberation is shared and we are bound together.

- The human spirit is made for generosity and it calls out the best of who we are.
- We can give without anything bad happening to our loved ones or to us.
- Sharing resources is life-giving for the receiver—and the giver.

We weave generosity into our company culture. We've created the generosity marketplace that allows our community members to give and receive the resources to do the work of sustainable abundance. This gives our clients the opportunity to "pay it forward."

We encourage you to *choose to give,* rather than to give based on what you might *get* in return for your "good deed." This choice allows us to create a positive, generous new story that helps us find our voice and declare, "I am enough."

practices
for law 2

Practice #1:

Mindfulness Practice

> Mindfulness means paying attention in a
> particular way: on purpose, in the present
> moment, and nonjudgmentally.
>
> **—Jon Kabat-Zinn**[16]

WHAT IS MINDFULNESS?

In its original form, mindfulness was part of the practice laid out by the Buddha that offered people a path from suffering to peace; from misunderstanding and misperception to a clear understanding of the nature of the human mind and how we suffer; and a clear path to liberation from our suffering.

The path includes ethical teachings and specific practices for cultivating a wise mind and an open heart—even in the face of violence and oppression.

This teaching of mindful awareness has caught secular attention for its very practical aspects: building one's ability to observe oneself and building one's capacity to pause before acting.

These skills lead us to see the possibility of thoughtfully responding rather than automatically reacting.

WHY PRACTICE MINDFULNESS?

With any new practice, we encourage an investigation into why we want to start. After all, we're investing our time and resources and want to know it will make a difference.

There are many scientific and anecdotal benefits to a regular mindfulness practice:

- We can realize that we are not our thoughts. Thoughts happen and we can notice which ones we wish to believe and which ones we can let go of.
- We can create a gentle, loving attitude toward ourselves— especially through times of transitions.
- We can soften our harsh judgments of self and others and invite a softening of our critical tone; this opening allows us to see each person's humanity, including our own, more clearly.
- We develop a calm serenity in the face of unfortunate circumstances, like when "bad things happen to good people."
- We find an easier stance with difficult emotions and body sensations, such as grief and pain.
- We develop a willingness to be transparent and address conflicts more readily.
- New neural pathways get built in the brain that allow us to access a calm and centered presence.

DOING IT "RIGHT"

To make a new habit, it's helpful to create conditions that encourage success.

Sometimes people get tripped up, wondering if they're "doing it right." A teacher of ours recently said, "If you are engaging in the practice, you are doing it right."

It also helps to know that the benefits can take a while to become apparent. Creating any habit requires practice and patience.

SET INTENTION FOR PRACTICE

Take a moment to recall why you are practicing: to gain self-awareness, to calm your nervous system, to build your capacity to focus in the face of the barrage of incoming information. Whatever the reason, bring it to mind as you begin your practice.

THE SPACE FOR PRACTICE

Set up a space that you will use for your mindfulness meditation. It might be a specific chair you find comfortable, or a more traditional setup with a cushion on the floor. You might wish to decorate this area in some way, although it's not necessary. Many of our clients sit in their office. Simply having a designated space for sitting quietly is enough.

Then pick a time of day to practice if you can. It's good for the body to have the consistency. Having a regular time means one less thing to decide each time you sit.

POSTURE FOR PRACTICE

You can meditate sitting on the floor or in a chair, standing, walking, or lying down; we encourage you to try all four postures to see what works best for you.

Basic posture for meditation has a few key ingredients: the body ought to be alert, open, and receptive, three fundamental qualities of yin. You want to have an upright position that opens your diaphragm so you can breathe deeply. Find the position that makes you feel alert yet relaxed. If you have physical pain in your posture it will make focus extra challenging.

The gaze is either downcast or with eyes closed.

THE BASIC PRACTICE

- Assume your posture.
- Set your intention for practice.
- Choose a focal point to feel your breath: at your nostrils, heart, or abdomen. Allow your attention to rest in that area of the body.
- With curiosity and interest, we begin to notice breathing in. Breathing out.
- Each time the mind wanders off—and *it will wander*—you simply call your attention back to each breath, with awareness and *kindness*.
- You may only be present to one or two breaths before your "monkey mind" wanders off. That's fine. Just notice and return as you can.
- You may silently repeat a gentle word when the mind wanders. Simply say to yourself, "thinking" or "planning" with no judgment. Keep inviting yourself back to the here and now each time you notice you have left. This practice is about returning over and over again, coming home when we leave— even if it's uncomfortable or unpleasant.

You may not notice the benefits of your mindfulness practice while engaged in the practice. Your mind will still continue to wander. It's not about getting "better."

Many people find the true impact of the practice comes after a few weeks of being out in the world.

We encourage you to begin by linking a new mindfulness practice to another established habit such as brushing your teeth, eating a meal, getting in the car or on the train for work.

Commit to pausing and paying attention to three full inhalations and exhalations of your breath. There is no need to breathe in a particular way, just pay attention to your breath. Once you build this breath practice up to several times a day, you may want to try sitting or standing for five minutes each day.

We recommend you work up to meditating twice a day in two ten-minute increments.

You can practice with us at the Seven Stones Leadership Mindfulness Group on the Insight Timer app (available on the iPhone app store and Google Play).

Practice #2:
Declaration

Simply repeat the following phrases as a mantra throughout the day. This can be part of a meditation or journaling practice. Think of them, or write them down—anytime.

I am enough.
You are enough.
We are enough.

Practice #3:
Experimenting with the Tools of Sufficiency

Whenever you feel the weapons of scarcity at play, stop and try to name which weapon has you trapped. Then choose a tool of sufficiency to deploy the moment you experience that particular weapon.

For example, if *comparison* is your weapon of choice, try choosing *generosity* as your tool. Then whenever you feel comparison you give something to someone.

The best way to find the tools that work best for you is to try several against the same weapon.

Practice #4:
Awareness of your Internal Monologue

When you wake up, notice what your first thoughts are. Are you focused on not enough?

Throughout the day, notice your thoughts when you are commuting to work or school, when your boss calls you in their office, when your mother calls or texts you. Are you trapped in the reverie of not enough?

If yes, notice and see if you can shift your dialogue.

Practice #5:
Cocreation Practice

Take a moment to sit back in your chair and find a comfortable position. You can lie down as long as you can stay alert. Let yourself be in a posture that is open and receptive. Connect to the back of your body so the front is soft and open.

As you're finding a comfortable position, let your breath begin to deepen. Use your inhale to gather energy and the exhale to ground and arrive in the body.

- What is it like to sit in a receptive posture?

- What do you notice? Does it feel safe, vulnerable, unsafe, new, familiar, difficult, easy?
- Do you notice any urge to lean forward or feel compelled to move into some kind of action? Just notice. See if you can remain in this soft, open, receptive posture for a few minutes. If not, it's ok, and, if so, just keep exploring what you find here.

Experimenting with Enough Time

Many of us are in scarcity around time. We never have enough to do the things we know to do or want to do. This practice is for you to experiment with your time: **Do not multitask. Do one thing at a time.** If you normally read the paper and eat breakfast at the same time, pick one or the other. If you email while on conference calls or watching a movie, only do one . . . you get the picture. No cell phones in the bathroom, no talking on the phone while driving. Do one and only one thing and while you're at it, *be* with the people in the room or on the phone with you.

Try this for an hour. Build up to a day, then a week.

What do you notice? How do you feel different? Was it hard to keep up? (Probably!) Did only doing one thing at a time give you a deeper experience of that thing? (Probably!)

We often multitask when we don't feel like we have enough time, but time feels different, more expansive, when we focus on a single thing.

Try it—and give yourself the gift of time.

law 3
i belong

Where have I truly belonged?

You belong. Period, full stop. No matter who you are or where you are from. Your story matters, you are enough and you belong, regardless of what you think or believe. As David Whyte eloquently writes, "There is no house like the house of belonging."[17]

So, how can we say that everyone belongs, unconditionally, without exception?

In the *story of enough*, you know that you belong because you are here. How can anyone or anything that is here on this planet *not* belong? Really?

Yet, we believe some of us don't belong. Some of us don't get a seat at the table. Who gets to decide? Who determines who's in and who's out: those who write the stories, of course. In our *story of enough*, each of us belongs. This is the undeluded truth of life on Earth.

In life, everything belongs and everything makes a difference to the collective whole. Take, for example, the gray wolf in Yellowstone National Park. The animals had been gone from the park for seventy years when they were reintroduced in 1995.

Due to the wolves' protracted absence, many things in the park had changed: with their primary predator gone, the numbers of deer and elk had exploded, reducing vegetation growth in huge areas of the park despite human efforts.

Even though only a small number were reintroduced, the effects were enormous. The wolves radically changed the behavior of the deer, who, with a predator nearby, began to move more. They grazed for less time in any one location, eating less vegetation. Trees and shrubs began to return. Birds returned when trees regrew. The number of beavers increased, using the new trees to build dams that produced habitats for other creatures. Otters and muskrats and ducks and fish reappeared. Wolves killed coyotes too. This meant that mice and rabbits grew in numbers, leading to more hawks and weasels and badgers. Ravens and eagles came down to feed on the carcasses wolves left. Bear populations grew.

This small pack of wolves even changed the course of rivers! Regenerating forests stabilized riverbanks. Pools formed, which created other habitats. No one knew beforehand that removing this one species would have a cascading effect on everything else in the park but it did.

In *The Hidden Connections*, Fritjof Capra reminds us, "In an ecosystem, no being is excluded from the network. Every species, even the smallest bacterium, contributes to the sustainability of the whole."[18]

Invisible as it can seem, we are like the gray wolf. Each of us is affecting the whole—even if we don't know how.

In the classic film *It's a Wonderful Life*, the hero, George Bailey, was given the chance to see what happened if he had never been born. The entire town and the lives of the people within it were changed, drastically and for the worse, because he wasn't there. Remove one being and it can have an enormous effect—even if we don't know what the effect will be.

And, yet, we humans have created stories of separation and alienation that lead directly to people experiencing a lack of belonging. Fritjof Capra explains the challenge: "In the human world of wealth and power, by contrast, large segments of the population are excluded from the global networks and are rendered economically irrelevant." Economic irrelevance is a slippery slope to personal irrelevance and not belonging. Yet wealth and power are not the only things that keep us separate.

The Myth of Separation

We may feel the separation and lack of belonging because our bodies don't fit some artificial cultural box. We may be too tall, too short, too thin, or too fat. We may be Jewish in a country of Muslims or Christian in a country of Hindus. Our skin color, hair texture, way of thinking and feeling, can all lead us to conclude that we are separate from those around us and therefore don't belong. Social mores may exacerbate our experience of separation and lack of belonging. Our gender identity, sexual orientation, marital status, illness, and history can all influence our sense that we don't have a place in our culture.

Almost no one feels like they belong in a society where what belonging looks like is mostly an illusion. As Sebastian Junger writes in *Tribe*, "Bluntly put, modern society seems to emphasize extrinsic values over intrinsic ones, and as a result, mental health issues refuse to decline with growing wealth. The more assimilated a person is into American society, the more likely they are to develop depression during the course of their lifetime, regardless of what ethnicity they are."[19]

The "Self-Made" Fallacy

Those of us in the United States have been living in a story of "the individual." This story claims anyone can make it. Anyone, that is, who works hard enough, sacrifices enough, and perseveres to overcome obstacles. And there are plenty of stories of those who have done just that. It is the heart of the American possibility.

The only problem is that it's only a tiny piece of the whole story. No one, absolutely no one, has made it on their own, which makes this story an explicit expression of the myth of separation.

This notion of the self-made man (person) is bogus, false at its core. All successful people had help: people who went out on a limb and supported their career, went to bat for them, bailed them out of trouble when it struck. Not to mention the huge debt we all have to the roads, bridges, and electrical infrastructures that are essential to every business.

Benjamin Franklin's autobiography was the first to tell a rag-to-riches story that uplifts the individual and ignores all of the support he had along the way to his success.

While Ben was "making it on his own," his sister, Jane, spent her life caring for their parents. Ben abandoned them and went on to do great things. She remained in her "station" taking care of those he had left behind.

Without her generosity and hard work, could he have accomplished everything he did? Brooke Gladstone, a journalist, talked about the myth of upward mobility on *On the Media*: "Ever since (referring to Ben Franklin's autobiography), the self-made man has been the avatar of the American spirit, especially in politics. Starting with 'Old Hickory' Andrew Jackson right up to Hillary Clinton citing her drape-making dad and Donald Trump claiming he grew his fortune from nothing but a 'small multimillion dollar loan from his father.'"[20]

Fast forward to the twenty-first century. In this era of perceived separateness and a pervasive mythology that "I alone can create my life," those of us who live amidst great affluence are probably less capable of caring for ourselves than any humans before us.

We're entirely dependent on technology: on electricity; on food being trucked in from distant farms; on so much man-made infrastructure that we'd have a tough time even doing basic things without it.

But people have always relied on things beyond themselves: on the bounty of nature for food; on animals for labor and food;

on their neighbors to exchange goods; and later, on a banking system to provide money for further trade.

We *all* owe a deep gratitude to the men and women who fought for the rights of freedom of speech, freedom of religion, freedom to gather that we have in Western society. We take so much for granted. It is a great triumph when we awaken to all who came before us to make our lives, such as they are, possible.

The Story of "Me"

This story is seared into the American psyche: the story of "me." It's the story of a person's rise to the top. Unfortunately, it's used to justify all manner of neglect for our fellow humans who are less capable of rising up out of their circumstances to live the American dream.

Yet we all rely on a vast network to support our modern, interdependent lives. We need others to help us when we're sick, grow our food, make our clothes, construct our homes, fix our cars, manufacture our computers and smartphones, build our networks, as well as keeping them running.

Scratch the surface of any perceived aloneness and there is life support everywhere. We recognize that the idea of loneliness and an existential sense of separateness have been present in human life for centuries now. Beginning, at least, with the teachings of the Buddha, human beings have been attempting to understand this break in belonging.

From philosophy to psychology, we attempt to make sense of the experience we have of being alone and separate. On our journey to sustainable abundance we reconnect with that which has been mythologized out of our minds, and reclaim the truth. And yet we can still feel separate.

We hear story after story from our clients who experience a profound sense of separation or "break in belonging" as children. We have those stories too, as an African American (Gina) and a Jew (Jen). We both experienced trauma and racial/religious bias. When Gina was in kindergarten she remembers:

> I was playing on the playground on a sunny day and I overheard two teachers talking. One asked, in what I heard was a pretty neutral tone, "Oh, how many black children are here at the school?" The other teacher responded, "One." I remember stopping my playing and looking down at my hand and touching my skin. I knew that they were talking about me. My first thought was, "I am different—I must not belong, I am alone."

For Jen:

> I got called names for being Jewish, had swastikas written on my notebook at school. Sometimes I got told, "We hate kikes, but you are OK." Mostly I felt endangered. I often wondered if Hitler would come back and take me away. By the time I was eleven or so I decided I did not want to be Jewish anymore.

Most of us have secrets we hide because we fear something is wrong with us. Unfortunately, by hiding them, we further separate ourselves and fuel our sense of being alone. Gina didn't come home from school that day and tell her parents what happened. She never spoke to them or anyone about it until she was an adult.

All of us have a moment or moments when we feel like we don't belong—it's one of the reasons we crave literature and drama—so we can see that our terrible fears and secrets aren't ours alone. Other people have them, too. Then we feel less alone.

No matter who we are, we share more in common than we don't. Rich or poor, female or male, gay or straight, every color, race, age, shape, and size—we want the same basic things! Love, safety, security, and to have a purpose.

We struggle to feel good about ourselves while pretending we feel great. We wonder why we are anxious and think it's only us. We are addicted to things that don't make us happy, and we hide it. We are not alone. We are not separate.

The Myth of Development

Larry Yang, a dear meditation teacher of ours, says, "We do not walk on this Earth. We are Earth that walks." Reconnecting to nature itself is another important aspect of belonging. We depend wholly on the dirt, air, sun, and rain to produce our nourishment and keep our bodies, the host of our consciousness, alive. Most of us, most of the time, forget this.

When we listen to what some Indigenous peoples can teach us, we see that they belong, have a sense of the sacred in all of life, and act in accordance. Exploring how they relate to the world can help us find our way back to an intimate connection to Mother Earth.

For example, in one Southeast Asian nomadic sea diving culture, the Moken, there are no known words for "hello" and "goodbye" or "mine" or "take" or "want." This group of people does not ever experience leaving one another or a sense that there is an "I" or "me" to protect. They live as if always connected, with no sense of separation, even when out of physical proximity to one another.

Ladakh is a community nestled high up in the western Himalayas. For most of its history, the people there experienced no domestic violence, no sexual abuse, no teen suicide, no alcoholism, and virtually no crime. Within fifty years of the introduction of modernization and Western ideals, domestic violence became a notable phenomenon. People began to need treatment for addiction and teens began to attempt suicide.

In her book, *Learning from Ladakh,* anthropologist Helena Norberg-Hodge documented the impact of Western ideals of development on this once thriving and happy people. Norberg-Hodge writes,

> When I first arrived in Ladakh the absence of greed was striking. As the development commissioner observed, people were not particularly interested in sacrificing their leisure or pleasure simply for material gain. The messengers of *development* . . . have implicitly been telling the Ladakhis that their traditional practices are backward and that modern science will help them stretch their natural resources to produce more than ever. Development is stimulating dissatisfaction and greed. Traditionally the Ladakhis had used the resources in their immediate vicinity with remarkable ingenuity and skill and worked out how to live in relative comfort and enviable security. They were satisfied with what they had. But now, whatever they have is not enough.[21]

It's important to call out that development is one of the sacred cows of the modern story. Development is good. Development is the way. Development will lift us all out of poverty and bring a great life to all peoples. Conversely, we have a prejudice against less "developed" peoples. What they have, in this modern quest for more, is not valuable, it's "less than" in some basic way.

The teachings of peoples who have known how to listen deeply to Earth's call are becoming more and more available to us. They remind us that the Earth is living and she is the source of all things, offered freely. As we wake up from our dream of separation and domination, these cultures have much to offer.

What can we learn from these sustaining cultures? How can we bring their mind-set into our world? An article titled, "We Were All Indigenous and Can Again Become" in the blog, *Unsettling America*, says,

> all of us have direct lineage to a different way of being, to a direct experience with the world. We once lived unmediated from the earth, ate directly from the forest, drank straight from its waters, slept touching the ground, healed ourselves with its plants, made all of our decisions concerning our lives with people we loved. We are still these people, only scarred. . . . We have been tamed. We have been domesticated. But, we are still connected under this baggage.[22]

Where have you been tamed? How is it working for you?

We Belong to Everything

We belong to everything. Always. It is fundamentally impossible not to, and no one, no matter how much power or status they hold, gets to tell you otherwise. Meditation teacher and best-selling author Sharon Salzberg says it like this: "It is only due to our concepts that we feel separate from the world. We are isolated by ideas of inadequacy, ideas of danger, ideas of loneliness, and ideas of rejection. In any given moment, do I choose to strengthen the delusion of separation or the truth of connection?"[23]

THE NEUROBIOLOGY OF BELONGING

Renowned psychologist Matthew Lieberman, author of *Social: Why Our Brains Are Wired to Connect,* used fMRI technology and neuroscience to reveal that our need to connect with other people is fundamental. Lieberman states, "Across many studies of mammals, from the smallest rodents all the way to us humans, the data suggests that we are profoundly shaped by our social environment and that we suffer greatly when our social bonds are threatened or severed. When this happens in childhood it can lead to long-term health and educational problems. We may not like the fact that we are wired such that our well-being depends on our connections with others, but the facts are the facts."[24]

Think for a moment of a new mom cooing at her baby. She makes those funny faces, speaks in a higher tone of voice, says things like "I see you. You are so cute. Yes, you are." She has that mama look on her face.

That baby talk is purposeful—it triggers things in the baby's brain. We have what scientists call "mirror neurons." In simple terms this means that being seen and then being mirrored is critical to our developing sense of self and connection.

If we don't get that kind of mirroring, we open ourselves to a host of feelings of aloneness and a sense of isolation. Without the mirroring, our brains don't make certain neural connections that help us grow into empathic, self-aware, sensing beings.

In his book *Mindsight,* Daniel Siegel, MD, writes, "Our resonance with others may actually precede our awareness of ourselves. Developmentally and evolutionarily, our modern self-awareness circuitry may be built upon the more ancient resonance circuits that root us in our social world."[25]

In conjunction with the way our brains grow, the human nervous system is influenced by other people's nervous systems. So, when a kind caregiver soothes an upset child, that child will have physiological changes. The child's heart rate will go down, their blood pressure drops, and the parasympathetic nervous system will get activated and allow that child to relax.

According to Thomas Lewis in *A General Theory of Love*, "A baby's physiology is maximally open-loop: without limbic regulation, his vital rhythms collapse, and he will die—as Rene Spitz proved. In current parlance, babies outsource more physiologic governance to parents and gradually bring those duties in house over months to years. Their early exposure to the external order that parents provide teaches babies how to manage some physiologic rhythms on their own."[26]

Pediatricians use the term "failure to thrive" to describe children left in orphanages or otherwise abandoned, neglected, or abused. Children who aren't touched, not mirrored, and not loved are shorter and often have psychological and physical issues that can become long term.

We are made to be in contact. We are designed to thrive in the company of others. We require love and contact to grow tall and strong and into our full humanness. But it doesn't stop when we reach a certain age. We require these connections through our entire lives. We never outgrow our need for love or contact. By adulthood, even when we're physically and emotionally secure, we still need each other for stability.

Lewis goes on to state, "Adults remain social animals; they continue to require a source of stabilization outside of themselves. That open loop design means that in some important ways, people cannot be stable on their own—not should or shouldn't be, but can't be. This prospect is disconcerting to many, especially in a society that prizes individuality as ours does. Total self-sufficiency turns out to be a daydream whose bubble is burst by the sharp edge of the limbic brain. Stability means finding people who regulate you well and staying near them."

It is tragic when we berate ourselves over a perceived lack of resolve or backbone because we "can't go it alone." Understanding our brain development helps explain why humans are designed to be in the presence of a loving tribe of some sort. How can we not trust millions of years of evolution? How can we not rest in the design of body and brain, heart and mind?

Reweaving the Web of Creation

Whatever affects one directly, affects all indirectly. I can never be what I ought to be until you are what you ought to be. This is the interrelated structure of reality.
—**Martin Luther King, Jr.**[27]

Community is a tapestry of the individuals and groups making up our lives as social beings. Part of the difficulty of our modern existence is that our impact on one another and our planet is easily obscured from our view.

For example, it is extremely difficult to directly feel the impact we create when we throw something in the trash. We are not usually aware of where it goes, what toxins get leached out of the trash, and where they end up. Said eloquently by environmental activist Julia Butterfly Hill, "We talk of throwing things away, but where is away?"[28] Away does not exist. Anything we dispose of is actually still here, having an impact. We think "away" is someplace that won't touch us. Until we feel an impact, such as having toxins in the water or children getting ill in clusters, it's almost impossible to see cause and effect in our world today.

When we recognize and become accountable for our belonging, we see there is no "away." Nothing and no one can be left out. This is the deep secret of our interconnection. Our suffering matters. Each person's suffering matters. Buddhist teacher and author Jack Kornfield speaks to it this way, "You can search the universe and not find a being more worthy of love than yourself."[29] We are equal in our belonging to this life.

Social Fabric: Torn and Repaired

Knowing our interdependence fosters a sense of wholeness and strengthens our connection to self and community. We live in a time where the underlying social fabric feels torn. We often take part in an activity as if we operate in a silo, independent of others. From this perspective, we are likely to engage in comparison, competition, winning/losing, and entertain other weapons of scarcity.

We see this all around us, like a friend reminiscing about how his family used to have dinner, "My whole family. Every Sunday, sometimes other nights. But now everyone works all the time. No one gets together anymore."

Jen experienced isolation and despair after having a baby. "Nursing was pretty uncomfortable, even painful. Many of my friends were without children and family was too far away to help.

When I reached out to the community, I found one agency who sent help for free. Everything else I needed cost money. Paying for help that would have at one time been part of the fabric of life added to my despair. I was both grateful to have resources and find help, and simultaneously, I felt alienated in having to pay a stranger for the help I wished I had gotten from within a robust social network."

What would a New American Dream be, one sourced from sustainable abundance? Already there are many signs of a returning to community awareness and a partnership with nature, not just to survive, but to thrive. Today, we see a call to community in cohousing developments, community gardens, time trade circles, Internet forums, and other subtler interactions.

What would it look like to accept, to know, and to live inside of our interdependence? To feel in our hearts and souls that we are one with all beings—plants, animals, the elements, and every human on this planet?

This requires two things: bringing our awareness to what already is, and the capacity to sense or feel the connection.

Reweaving the web of creation is an ongoing practice. It requires recognition of what's underneath the myths of separation, then engaging in actions that strengthen that recognition.

Social fabric is the intersection of community and interdependence, knowing we matter and understanding how deeply we were made to belong. Social fabric is, in part, the structure of relationships that kept us connected and cared for.

For our grandparents, it was our neighborhood, extended families, our church or temple that grounded our daily life. These were the communities that uplifted us during hard times and celebrated the good times. As a culture, we had a sense of our interdependence then. The connections between the generations acted as a reminder that we were not on our own.

When our neighbor's husband died, it impacted the whole community. Social fabric has to do with people knowing each other, knowing that their lives are intertwined, and taking the time and space to connect to one another.

Mattering

So how do we help restore our social fabric? By knowing that we are part of it—and we matter. What if your absence was not just noticed but keenly felt?

Despite what you might think, your absence *is* felt. It can cause other people to feel disappointed, neglected, even angry.

Yes, we sometimes need to make a choice that will piss off someone else. We have to choose between family and work, or work and friends. Fine. Just don't pretend it doesn't matter. It does. You matter. Be responsible for it.

But then we often tell ourselves, "They won't miss me." Life goes on. On one level that's true. But on a deeper level, your absence matters. It may truly be unavoidable, but it still matters.

What if we know who we are for others and that we are always making a difference? What if we completely and totally matter and all voices count? Then what do our communities look like, sound like, act like?

Not only do we matter, we require each other in order to thrive. We require each other to be seen.

Our knowledge that we matter is part of this social fabric. Each of us has been in a group, and we can feel how the group is changed when one person is missing. Sometimes we are relieved by their absence and sometimes we mourn it. Regardless, it has an impact. That is what it means to matter.

There is a famous Basotho tale that was modified into a play about apartheid. In the play, the dragon-monster Kodumodumo has gobbled up the whole Basotho nation. This act made him so enormous that he got stuck in the high mountain passes. Of all the people in the world only one, Senkatana, survived. He was alone. He could do what he liked, he was free, but in a great voice he wailed:

I cannot find myself
because I am not among others

about what shall I be happy if I am only by myself?
from what shall I be freed if it is only me?

why would something be beautiful
if only my eyes are seeing it?

it is you who are calling forth the I
it is I who imagines himself through you
the you imagines me

I do not choose you
that you are there makes me

we have been made to be with others
or we will be hungry amidst great abundance[30]

practices
for law 3

Practice #1:
Community Inventory

- What do I consider my community?
- What does my current community look like?
- Who is in my community? What groups, organizations, institutions, buildings, structures, activities, shared purposes make up what I call my community, or my communities?
- Who is outside of my community? Why are they not a member?
- How is this community, or these communities, enough?
- How does my community nourish me? How do I nourish it?
- What are the roles I play?
- How has my relationship changed with my community as I have aged?
- Are there actions for me to take inside of my communities?
- Is there a community I am ready to leave? Or one I am ready to enter?
- What have I discovered or rediscovered about my relationship to community or social fabric?
- Do I understand that I matter?

Practice #2:

Taking Up Your Rightful Space

Stand up and get as tall as you can with your feet planted firmly on the ground. Let your knees be loose, not locked.

Take deep, full breaths. On your exhales, let your jaw and shoulders relax. As you lift up the torso and open the crown to the sky, feel your length.

Let yourself feel your feet. Imagine now that from your feet grow roots that burrow down into the earth.

Continue to breathe fully as you sense the force of gravity on your body. Let the inhales lift you tall, while the exhales soften you down.

Sense gravity. Sense earth.

Now notice your energy field and make it equal in all directions: front, back, left and right, above and below.

Feel your width. Keep breathing.

Notice if there is a dimension that is more difficult to feel or inhabit: perhaps in the back, the throat, below the feet, or somewhere else. Using the breath and your attention to direct energy, extend your energy there. Widen it. Have those width dimensions be equal side to side so you have enough room for all of you to exist, to be. Keep breathing and softening.

Send energy and attention down while lengthening up and expanding out in all directions. Now notice your back space and front space. We so often lose contact with what is behind. Feel it now. Who or what is at your back? Who or what has your back? Notice the space in front too. The future as it extends in front of you. Balance in the dimensions. Do this for any amount of time.

Practice #3:
I Belong Declaration

Whenever you find yourself thinking that you are different, that you don't belong, or that you are an imposter, this simple declaration practice over time can make a difference. Regardless of the circumstance—meeting, dinner party, job interview—silently repeat the phrase: "I belong, I know I belong because I am here."

Practice #4:
We Are

Go outside.
    Face the sun or the moon.
    Rest quietly.
    Breathe deeply.
    Feel your world around you, feel the ground beneath you.
    Read these words out loud or to yourself:

        If my neighbor is hungry, I am hungry.
        If my neighbor is joyful, I am joyful.
        If my neighbor is homeless, I am homeless.
        If my neighbor is beautiful, I am beautiful.
        If my neighbor is lonely, I am lonely.
        If my neighbor is vibrant, I am vibrant.
        This is my neighborhood.

My community.

We are interdependent.

We are one.

Now take a few minutes with these questions:

- What did you notice?
- What resonates?
- Where could you feel or sense connection and depth?
- Where does this still just sound like a nice idea?
- What would it take to thaw any numb or frozen places in you that do not yet "know" this oneness?

Practice #5:
Meet Your Neighbors

We have been surprised to discover how many people do not know their neighbors. They have lived for years in a home and don't know the person right next door. Here are a few experiments that can get you out to meet your neighbors:

- Invite your neighbor over for a cup of tea or a glass of wine one Saturday afternoon.
- When you are walking your dog, pause and introduce yourself to your fellow dog walker.

- Create a progressive dinner night.*
- Create a neighborhood soup.**
- Attend a few of your neighborhood watch, town council, or local political meetings.

---

*A progressive dinner is when several families agree to host the neighbors for dinner. The first family serves appetizers then the party moves to the second family that serves salad, then main course, etc.

**In Gina's former Westville neighborhood in New Haven, CT, over the winter they would have Sunday Soups. Here's how it works: Sunday Soup runs from 6 pm to 8 pm. Hosts will provide the soup and everyone will bring their own soup cups, spoons, and something to share (beverage or tasty treat). The hosts often make mac and cheese for the kids and the variety of soups take into consideration · vegans, vegetarians, and omnivores. Anyone in the neighborhood is invited.

law 4
no one is exempt

When I let go completely, what will become of me?

On a cold winter day in New England, Jen's husband was upstairs resting after another hellish day of cancer treatment. Jen was standing outside shoveling. Her husband normally plowed the long driveway. The heavy snow hurt her back. With each shovelful she could hear herself asking, "Why me? Why, after everything I have done, all my work, all my good deeds, why is all this happening to me?"

She was having a little pity party. Then, like a flash, she heard another voice ask, "Why *not* you? What makes you so special? Why should this *not* be happening to you?" Spouses with cancer are less than a rare phenomenon so what made her think she was exempt from the vicissitudes of life that affect us all?

She could see how, beneath her conscious awareness, she had been thinking that if she was good, if she did her meditations, was a good mom, did good work, that she would get some kind of safety in the storm. Her life of good and moral actions would be traded for some kind of free pass from this brush with death or even from death itself.

Until that moment, she wouldn't have believed she'd bought into this quid pro quo so embedded in our social and religious traditions. Yet clearly that story was in there, somewhere, driving actions in a way she was wholly unaware of until just then.

We have been sold a bill of goods. We are told that if we work hard, have a family, and do good things for the world we will be rewarded. With what? Good question. A ticket to heaven? Insulation from the horror "other" people face? Many of us make a deal with the devil and don't even know it. Here is how the bargain sounds: "If I do all sorts of transformation work, if I evolve myself, if I go to workshops, use the law of attraction, clear my chakras, pray well, go to my church, synagogue, mosque, or temple, do my work, then somehow, some way, the things that happen in other people's lives, won't happen in mine. Magically all this work will make me exempt from . . . well . . . anything bad." But being good doesn't give you a pass. It doesn't work that way for *anybody*.

Our modern Western society promotes the idea of exemption. If we follow a certain diet, do certain exercises, and live a certain way . . . if we say enough prayers, do enough good deeds. If, if, if . . . then we can defy, outwit, or at least delay old age, illness, and maybe even death! When we say it out loud we all know it's nonsense but look closely and see if maybe you, too, think that if you play your cards just right, you will be exempted from suffering.

Gina likes to say, "No one is exempt, not even me." None of us are exempt from sickness, old age, and death. Gina learned this lesson when her grandfather died. He was part of what Tom Brokaw named "the greatest generation." He earned a Purple Heart, a Bronze Star, and was one of the few black majors in the desegregated Army. Yet he still got sick and died.

Upon his death, Gina realized that she had carried a belief that she didn't think she was going to die. "I'm a smart cookie, I'll figure my way out of this," was an unconscious belief she held.

When she saw the toughest man she knew succumb to dementia and death, she realized that she too could not escape. "Not even me."

We use Gina's insight as an exercise; we say to ourselves, *"No one is exempt, not even me."* This has become a simple practice that helps break up the delusions we face every day.

In one of our courses, a woman who was working with this came to a profound revelation, "If I am not exempt from the difficulties, I am also not exempt from the joys and delights of being alive." Very true.

This is one of those moments where we can call on our gratitude practice. Life is full of blessings large and small. Fruit all juicy and sweet. Waterfalls. The kindness of strangers. Our children. A teacher who noticed us when no one else did. Flowers. Poetry. The smell of yummy food.

The starker our circumstances, the deeper we may need to dig to find the blessings. Caroline Myss, author and spiritual teacher, likes to say, "It's easy to be grateful at a banquet."

We get to practice more rigorously when times are tougher. No matter how easily our brains focus on what is not working, what we do not have, we also have the power to focus on what is here, now.

PRACTICE: COUNT YOUR BLESSINGS

Pause right now and count your blessings. Set a timer for one minute and write or say what you're grateful for—for the whole minute—without stopping.

The Great Inversions

We've made some unfortunate inversions in our society. Instead of simply feeling worthy themselves, some people make others feel less worthy. Rather than recognizing that we are finite, we've created a profound sense of scarcity about the things that are infinitely available.

INVERSION #1: LETTING GO OF ENTITLEMENT

In 1948 the United Nations issued a Universal Declaration of Human Rights that set out, "for the first time, fundamental human rights to be universally protected...." These rights include but are not limited to: "the right to life, liberty, and security of person," being "entitled to equal protection of the law," "freedom of thought," and "the right to work . . . to rest and leisure."[31]

Yet in the scarcity story these fundamental human rights get chipped away and a shadow side of our rights arises. In our belief that we are exempt, we start to think we are entitled to be above or separate from others. We are not suggesting that human beings ought not to have human rights. We are suggesting that rights can sour into a sense of entitlement that justifies all manner of scarcity driven behavior.

One example is people who are rude to servers at restaurants—they think they're paying good money and are entitled to what they expect! And if they don't get it, they are entitled to berate the staff. No. They aren't exempt from common decency, nor do they have any right to abuse another person.

Another example is customer support—we pay a lot for our devices, shouldn't they always work perfectly? And if they don't, aren't we entitled to yell at the technical support people? Of course not. They're people, doing their jobs as well as they can.

We all have bad days—both as the ones doing the serving, and the ones being served—but *nobody* is entitled to be a jerk to someone else.

We all want to be treated humanely by individuals, groups, and governments. With the simple "do unto others" in mind, we can remind ourselves we *aren't* entitled to treat others any less than we want to be treated.

We also aren't entitled to things—a house or a car, a career . . . not even to health and happiness! These expectations feed the entitled scarcity story and support the delusion that we are unique and, therefore, especially deserving.

If we drop our expectations, entitlement can fall away and we can find a place where we can be deeply grateful for that which we do have. There is a great scene in the movie *The Best Exotic Marigold Hotel* where one person is asking another, "Why do you love India so much?" and the other answers, "Because, in India, people see life as a privilege and not a right."[32]

Entitlement and gratitude cannot inhabit the same space. The former occludes the latter, casting a shadow over its steady luminous glow. Entitlement lives in the story of separation. Gratitude comes straight from the well of sufficiency.

INVERSION #2: OUR STRUGGLE WITH FINITUDE

We are *all* finite and we are *all* going to die. It isn't fair. Or maybe it is.

The great equalizer for all beings is our inevitable death. Life is "too short." However much time we have, we ask for just one more day, one more moment.

Not accepting the truth of death leads us to be stuck in the sea of scarcity. We have the potential to see clearly—to recognize that the whole journey is precious and weird and empty and full all at once.

Our colleague, Paul Dunion, therapist, teacher, and author, once said, "Life is fundamentally out of control, mysterious, and dangerous." The ends to which we have gone as a society to deny this reality are astounding. And worse, they are making us sick, unhappy, emaciated, fat, and living way beyond our means personally and collectively.

We invite you to wonder with us about the connection between Western culture's misuse of finite resources and our collective denial of our own finitude. We are born and we die. Love is unconditional and limitless but relationships are not; they are full of conditions and limitations. Energy at a soul level is infinite and our consciousness represents that limitlessness, yet we inhabit bodies with great limitations that have finite time in this form.

One of the difficulties is that much of what is infinite is also part of the mystery. It cannot be seen or measured with the naked eye so we have been trained to miss or devalue it.

Perhaps, with curiosity, attention, humor, and other laws of enough, we might find peace and a way through life, even in the face of death.

The good news is that our fears, and the things that trigger us, can be the very portals to our freedom. If we can sustain attention on our fears, especially a great one like the very ending of our life and the finitude of everything we know to be real, we can experience freedom.

Directly facing the truth of our own impermanence gives us access to preciousness, fragility, deep caring, and universal love. In developing an accurate relationship to that which is finite, we produce an opening, giving us access to that which is truly infinite, experiences like love, joy, peace, ease, and, of course, sufficiency.

Every Day Is a Bonus Day

When Gina was in her early thirties, she worked at a telecommunications company. She had a coworker, white and male who was in his twenties. Gina reports, "There was something different about him. I couldn't put my finger on it. He seemed to be in the flow of life. Nothing seemed to worry him—but it wasn't from a place of privilege or entitlement. I couldn't figure out what was different about him." One day Gina went to lunch with him. He shared that he'd been mugged in Washington, D.C. late one night. His attackers shot him and left him for dead on the sidewalk.

"Every day is a bonus day," he said.

People who've faced their own mortality and lived can have a profoundly different experience of life. They can live with a deep and abiding knowledge that life is precious and no moment is guaranteed to anyone.

That means, "Every day is a bonus day," for all of us. Every single day. When we wake up and remember that today is a bonus we're lucky to get, the day has a better start.

In one of our workshops we did a practice of facing our own death. Everyone was told that they were going to die that day. Each person had the opportunity to write or call the people with whom they needed to speak. Each person had the opportunity to lie down, get covered with a blanket, and experience the end. We ushered them into, as the poet Mary Oliver says, "that cottage of darkness."[33] No more worry. No more striving. No more accumulation of resources for some future or for the children. No more ruminating about the past or the present. No more of anything.

Take a moment here. Notice what that possibility feels like.

After the exercise was over, people reported that facing into death was freeing, clarifying, and led to an immediate sense of release from burden. Some participants wrote letters of love and forgiveness and others heard their deepest callings.

In certain Buddhist lineages, monks spend a great deal of time pondering impermanence. Facing "what is so" produces what is often referred to as "the sure heart's release." This corrects the inversion our society has made by privileging that which is visible, tangible, and material over all else including our well-being.

Getting Ourselves Right Side Up

If you don't take care of yourself, you can't take care of others. It's all too easy to take from our own energy reserves more quickly than we can restore and recalibrate.

This sometimes-chronic lack of self-care is intertwined with misunderstanding our impermanence and our powerful desire to deny the truth of our own death.

We all do this in one way or another: promising more than we can deliver; inaccurately gauging how much time it will take us to fulfill tasks; and juggling more than we really have time for.

One rampant manifestation of this is a common inability to say "no" to anything. Ever had that happen? People cite a fear of missing out (fomo) or a sense that if I decline something, everything will go away, including our livelihood.

But if we're not conscious in our decisions, we end up with exactly what we feared—we miss out on being alert and present because our minds are elsewhere. Creating clear priorities helps you say "no" to things that aren't important to you. This frees up your time and energy for more important things.

Taking Great Care

When you take on too much, you get too little sleep.

Gina tried a sleep experiment because she felt exhausted all the time. She decided to stop setting her alarm and allowed herself to awaken in her own natural rhythm. She discovered that her energy was tied to hours of daylight and in the winter months she needed additional sleep to feel better.

Taking great care means being aware of the ever-changing rhythms of the world—and inside you. Pay attention to what your body is trying to tell you. If you're tired, you need sleep, not just more coffee or other artificial stimulants, which can make you feel worse in the end.

When you're aware, you are present to your limitations, desires, and needs.

Letting Go and Mourning

We've all experienced how hard it can be to let go. That's because we mourn the loss of things—even if we no longer want or need them. We mistakenly look at letting go as a loss, rather than freeing.

"The devil *we know* is better than the devil *we don't know*." Most of us have heard that saying. It is grounded in our neurology. As biological beings, we like equilibrium. We are programmed for homeostasis, so change, even positive change, requires a disruption of our much-prized patterns.

Trying to shift to a new paradigm that will relieve our long-term suffering can cause suffering in the short-term.

As we work with Law 4, we typically discover we must let go of our addictions to hoarding, distraction, comparison, and shame (or any other scarcity weapon). Letting go of anything in our lives—habits, stories, things, people—engages us in our resistance to change.

George Leonard, author of *Mastery: The Keys to Success and Long-Term Fulfillment,* says it this way, "The resistance here (as in other cases) is proportionate to the size and speed of the change, not whether the change is a favorable or unfavorable one."[34]

There are many sensations that come along during times of change and letting go. We may feel disoriented and confused, disenchanted, and disidentified. We may experience the physical sensations of pain, frustration, anxiety, surprise, sadness, and more.

Change requires letting go of how things *were then*, and adjusting to how things *are now*, which in many cases is laden with uncertainty.

It is often said that the one constant in life is change. Our colleague Shea Adelson says, "Developing the capacity to be with the uncertainty and continuing flow of change is an act of sufficiency because it allows us to be in reality with what is, and to open to what arises moment to moment."

When you think about letting go, you may ask yourself, "What do I have to give up?" Almost instantly we are grasping and holding on. It's normal and natural to feel this way, to anticipate some kind of deprivation or trepidation about the changes that might be coming.

Yet even wonderful changes can come with loss. In William Bridges' *Managing Transitions: Making the Most of Change,* he declares that our transitions start with an ending.[35] Getting married means losing the freedoms we had when we were single. Birthing or adopting or fostering children means letting go of another kind of freedom and reallocating all kinds of resources to care for the young ones. Moving to a great new place means saying goodbye.

Necessary losses are something everyone faces. There are losses we must face when we migrate from scarcity and excess to a life of sustainable abundance.

Getting Complete

There is clarity that comes from recognizing our impermanence. Getting complete is how we can enact that clarity of mind.

Knowing we will not go on forever we get complete so when our number is called we have little to no unfinished business. We are free to go.

Completing is not the same as ending. We end many things with which we are not complete. To be complete means to have left nothing unsaid; nothing unattended to or cared for; nothing festering so it can take even one ounce of your attention. It's a high bar to set and it's a clear way of honoring ourselves, our colleagues, our friends and families, and our organizations.

Many of us think of completion as finishing, ending, or stopping something. However, completing is something distinct from that. Completion is more like a process of emptying and taking stock of what's happened (or not).

When we complete something, we clear away any stuckness and move on without carrying anything forward unnecessarily or unwittingly. In completing, we give ourselves—and others—the opportunity to reflect and say anything that needs to be said. We take actions that may cause us to feel at ease with what has happened (or not) in our conversations, relationships, practices, intentions, etc.

Completion is part of letting go and offers us freedom. With this newfound freedom, new opportunities arise. It is no accident that at the end of a high school or college experience there is a commencement ceremony. From this place of completion and acceptance, we make room for something new.

Yet, we must not rush toward this space of discovery, toward new possibility or partnerships. In the laws of enough we appreciate waiting and not knowing as gifts of sustainable abundance.

Waiting and Not Knowing

Letting go of anything causes a disruption. So, learning to pause and *not know* what is next is a key skill to cultivate on our journey. Tolerating disruption, even welcoming it, is a competency we must have to create a life of sustainable abundance.

When we let go, we enter the "fertile void" and from this nothingness, possibilities abound. One of the original members of our Boston team, Kristi, recalls when she and her then-husband faced splitting up. "When the suffering stopped around what we were *not*, and we could rest in what we *were*, and what we could be . . . it held us."

Letting go of what they were supposed to be and how they were supposed to design their lives opened up a space of creation. The judge in their divorce and custody hearing said, "I want to acknowledge and thank you for what you have done." In the letting go they could come together and be what they already were: a family—just a different configuration of family. Kristi credits her work on the Boston sufficiency team for their ability to create such an outcome.

When we find ourselves completing, letting go, or in a place of not knowing, we often have the urge to fill the space quickly. We *add* more of something else, *anything* else, to make us feel better about what is happening. Or, we may even return to something familiar—the way things were.

Bridges states, "We don't let go of anything important until we have exhausted all the possible ways that we might keep holding on to it." We mostly do this unconsciously, so it's helpful to be aware of this human tendency as we pass through a transition or time of letting go.

Let's ask ourselves, "Am I trying to fill this void?" Bridges calls this void the *neutral zone,* "because it is a nowhere between two somewheres." And he declares it is "a very difficult time."

See how long you can let yourself be in *nowhere.* It's a fertile void, rich with possibility. Waiting is such a challenge in a culture that teaches us to grab every opportunity and seize every moment. It's an act of sufficiency to wait. Let there be nothing for a while. Relax into it and rest. Through that rest comes a profound experience of enough.

practices
for law 4

Practice #1:

I Am Not Exempt

Gina wrote the poem below, while contemplating Law 4. We offer it for
you to write your own list and to investigate for yourself what it would
mean if you knew that you were not exempt from death.

I AM NOT EXEMPT

If I *knew* I was not exempt,

If I *knew* I was going to die,

Become a frail old lady

Would I change how I lived my life?

I would:

Run more.

Eat less.

However, drink more wine and eat more chocolate.

Pay attention to the sun, moon, and stars.

Pay less attention to interest rates, 401Ks, and my children's dat-
ing lives.

Breathe deeper.

Laugh longer.

Sing out loud.

Dance in public.

Get rid of things.

Buy my dream car.

Visit all fifty states.

Throw more parties.

Watch less TV.

Read more books.

Email less.

Write more.

Sit in more hot springs.

Snowshoe.

Forgive easier.

Let go faster.

Love broader.

Take more baths.

Hug more trees.

Rub my stomach along the grass.

Spend more time naked, wrapped in warm blankets.

Make one more snow angel.

Practice #2:
Letting Go

We let go all the time, when we fall asleep at night, when we get off the phone or move away or leave a job. Letting go allows change to take hold. Let's relax right now and ready ourselves to receive and allow whatever arises out of this practice.

Find a comfortable place to sit with enough support. Choose one where you won't be too hot or cold, it won't be too bright or dark—it feels just right. Make yourself as comfortable as possible.

Notice your breath and allow it to move freely in . . . out . . . and with each breath softening down your shoulders, relaxing your jaw and any tension in your upper back, and letting your breath to continue to be free and easy, not doing anything with it.

As you exhale, let go of any tension in the body that's ready to be released. Continue to breathe and relax, settling more and more deeply into your chair. This in and of itself is a letting go.

Allow yourself to notice a part of yourself that is extremely comfortable, even more comfortable than the rest of you.

Now let yourself connect with a loss from your life.

Bring that loss into your mind's eye and notice the shape, the color, the texture, the images or sounds, or temperatures, or edges, anything about the loss that comes up.

Bring it to life through your imagination. It could come as words, images, or sounds. Now notice what beliefs and associations are part of that loss. What are the beliefs, hopes, fears, dreams that come with that loss? What did you have to give up?

Take a few breaths. Find your anchor. Now gather that loss, gather all the components of the loss. Package it up, in a gold ball of light. Take all the time you need to bring it together in a way that works for you. Do that now. Notice whatever arises as you gather it together and as you hold it.

Now, let it all go. Take that package and release it. You can give it to the earth; let it be absorbed into the ground. You can throw it into the ocean; leave it on a mountaintop. Whatever form of letting go comes to you, do that now.

What spontaneously arises as you invite the letting go?

Now come back to the body. Come back to your breath. What do you notice? What sensations or feelings, what new images, what is arising?

Just take notice. You might have a sense that the loss is present, or some part of it is present. That is OK. You might be present to your breath. You might be present to a deeper kind of emptiness or nothingness. You may feel relieved. Whatever is here is just fine.

This feeling you might be experiencing of sadness, emptiness, or nothingness is often the one that we move quickly to fill up. We might use food or sex or more spiritual development or more stuff, more relationships, anything to fill it up.

Emptiness can be awkward. Notice what is happening inside of whatever emptiness was created when you let go.

It is out of this emptiness that true creation is born. Feel it now. Embrace it as much as you can in complete honor of what is happening. And as we end this meditation, know that we will work with this fertile void of creation. Inside of the sufficiency practice we allow creation, we don't force creation. It can't be forced.

Take some time now to journal about your experience.

1. What insights or discoveries did you have about your loss?
2. How was it to let go? Was it easy, hard, impossible?
3. Is there anything left to let go of about it? If so, what steps would you like to take to do so?
4. What surprised you about this process?

Practice #3:
Inquiry for Letting Go

- What are you letting go of right now? Could be a relationship, a habit, a place, a thing or something else?

- What changes are you experiencing that you did not ask for? How do you feel about them?
- How have these times of uncertainty impacted your ability to attend to yourself? How do you nurture yourself when you are feeling stress and uncertainty?
- How do you know when it is time to let go and move on? What holds you back?
- What do you have to let go of to make room for something new? What would you have to let go of to experience a greater sense of community, purpose, commitment, truth, wisdom, joy, or love?
- What is arising from the space created from investigating finitude and letting go?
- How will you let go? What are you learning about this art of surrender and release? What possibilities are available to you today?

Practice #4:
Getting Complete

This format comes directly from Radical Therapy and Transactional Analysis work initiated in the 1970s and carried forward most prominently by Marshall Rosenberg and now called Nonviolent Communication. We encourage you to visit the Nonviolent Communication website for the rich resources that are available.[36]

There are several elements to *completing*. We need to be willing to:

1. **Speak the truth** as we see it.

2. **Listen to the other** with the intention to understand; not to blame, judge, or prove we are right.
3. **Be responsible** for our part in the matter. Or said another way, it takes two to tango.
4. **Let go** of what we are holding onto. Not so easy, but nonetheless critical for completing anything.

Specifically, we can follow a conversation "map" when we are afraid to say something that feels difficult. We follow a pattern of expressing what we **observe, feel, think,** and **request.** This allows us to share openly and be responsible for our own feelings and thoughts, while at the same time attempting to find out what is occurring for the other person.

We recommend trying this out first by practicing with someone you feel comfortable with and about something that is not too charged. Then it can flow more easily during a more challenging moment.

In general, we speak these statements in this order, but it is not necessary to be exact.

1. **When you...** (facts we observed).
2. **I feel...** (feelings *only*). This part can become a major pitfall in the pattern. Often, we will say, "I feel *like you*...." When we say that, or something like it, we are framing a thought inside of the disguise of a feeling statement. Instead of expressing a vulnerability of feeling—which includes sad, mad, hurt, anxious, afraid, etc.—we are making an assessment of the other person, typically causing defensive reactions and beginning a new cycle of communication breakdown. For this reason, the distinction of *feeling* matters a lot when we wish to understand deeply how communication has run amok.

3. **My interpretation/thoughts/read/paranoia/story is** . . . **because I saw/observed you** . . . (thoughts). It is here we express our assessments, true or not, and then include our observation and state the evidence if we haven't yet.

4. **The grain of truth in what you said is** . . . (acknowledgment). This may require some stretching on the part of the listener. At first pass, you may say nothing about what they think is true, but in this model, we stand behind the idea that no matter how triggered and distorted things can get between parties, there is some grain of truth that can be acknowledged by the other party that will have the upset person feel acknowledged and understood; like what they are feeling and thinking makes sense even if it's being colored by leftover material from the past littering the landscape of this current conversation.

law 5
resting is required

When was the last time I felt deeply rested?

In the scarcity story, there is never time to rest. We are constantly running, moving, striving, competing, making sure the other guy does not get too far ahead or we do not get too far behind.

We're overwhelmed with excess and too rarely let ourselves stop and restore. In our current "twenty-four-hour work cycle" society, we're leaving millions of hours of vacation time on the table every year. Even if we do go on vacation, we still read email, check in with the office, and sit in on a few calls.

Enough! If we can't find our own answer to the question, "What is enough?" then nothing can be.

Our body is our home. If we live like the house is on fire all the time, we miss the most basic sense that things are okay, right here, right now.

So how do we relax and have the sense of peace and ease we long for?

Resting in the Nervous System

The body is the place for us to build a foundation of basic rest. For our purposes, let's talk about the two main components of the nervous system: the sympathetic and the parasympathetic.

The sympathetic nervous system is designed for us to respond quickly under pressure. This is most often spoken about as our "fight, flight, or freeze" response. We are alert to danger and act quickly should danger appear on the horizon. These responses can be lifesaving.

The parasympathetic nervous system is often referred to as "rest and digest" or the "relaxation response." It is the part of the nervous system that slows us down, allows us to catch up to ourselves, relax and renew.

Our system is designed to be in rest and digest *most of the time,* allowing for short spurts of sympathetic activity that enables us to move quickly when in danger.

But in today's world, we tend to overuse our sympathetic system. We keep it on high alert from past and present threats too much of the time, and spend too little time in rest and digest. With fear and adrenaline pumping through our systems, slipping into scarcity is almost inevitable.

We face real health consequences from our extended stay on high alert. We suffer by rarely being rested or getting the sense that we are held by anyone or anything. According to the research of Richard Boyatzis, coauthor of *Resonant Leadership*, women in the West experience eight to fifteen chronic, annoying stress episodes a day.[37]

Stress and Cognitive/Emotional Impairment

The body responds to these stress episodes as trauma. The sympathetic nervous system wakes up and sends signals to the brain; hormones are activated. We automatically and unconsciously start to defend ourselves and we become cognitively and emotionally impaired.

Our peripheral vision drops. We can't handle complex tasks. We aren't open to new ideas. We can't think outside of the box. Sound familiar? These are the complaints we hear from many of our clients about themselves and/or their teams.

One problem is that we've confused true rest with fun activities. Watching movies, eating, drinking, and partying are fun. And, fun is necessary (see Law 6). They are not, however, what provides real nourishment and restoration to the human body and spirit.

Boyatzis specifies activities that provide real renewal:

- Meditation. It does not matter what kind.
- Yoga—any yoga that is restorative and moderate.
- Prayer to a loving God.

- Exercise at a moderate pace.
- Volunteering if you are not already in one of the help-
  ing professions.
- Noncombative martial arts, like tai chi.
- Petting an animal.
- Being hopeful about the future.
- Laughter, play, and joyfulness.

When we activate the relaxation response and return to the parasympathetic state of rest and digest, we send a simple and profound message to ourselves that *we're okay right now.*

Resting in Each Other

While there's a lot we can do for ourselves, there's also a lot we
can do for each other.

Jen had a client, Frank, on the massage table. They were doing
deep unwinding work. Jen held Frank's head in her hands and
asked him to let her carry the weight of his head and neck. She
said, "You don't have to hold yourself up alone. *I've got you.*"
Suddenly, without warning, he began to cry, hard. "No one,"
he said through the tears, "has ever had me." Almost within an
instant, his neck muscles softened. He relaxed into Jen's hands.
His whole body and mind softened. Once he dropped the feeling
of being alone and isolated, he could allow his parasympathetic
nervous system to take over and let him truly rest.

We've all had negative experiences with other people. It can
seem like a distant dream or a fantasy to relax into another. But it
is possible. Just as Frank relaxed into Jen's hands, each of us can
relax into our shared community of support and friendship.

For those who have had trouble in their early family situations, finding our tribe becomes critical to our well-being and ongoing ability to rest. That community might be a healing community, a hobby community, a friendship circle, a self-created family, a community based on our ethnicity, sexual orientation, or religious and spiritual connections.

Even after having been hurt, most of us reach out and find a community. It's built into us. We know at the deepest level that finding safe harbor is critical to our thriving. Together, we reweave the fabric of our interdependent lives.

Resting in the Grand Design

Life is full of paradox—so many opposing forces interacting. Opposites are a basic part of life's design. Let's ask ourselves how it might help us rest if we accept and work with them.

These forces, at odds, rubbing up against each other, are inviting us to struggle and grow beyond the opposition to deeper integration, unity, and reunion. Our teacher Suzanne Roberts calls it "the dynamic tension between two poles." "There is unity," she says, "at the center of opposites."

It is the light and the dark. The yin and the yang. In our culture, we have such a strong preference for eliminating one half of the equation. Only the light please. Only the happy please. Only the sun and not the rain. The Zen master says, "The Great Way is not difficult for those who have no preferences."

What if we make room for both? The shadow and the light can guide us equally toward our deepest rest. Once we give up exempting ourselves, face our impermanence completely, and let go, we can rest within the grand design instead of fighting it.

The Buddhist teachings speak to eight dynamic tensions, called the vicissitudes, through which we all cycle: gain/loss, fame/disrepute, praise/blame, and pleasure/pain.[38] Whether we are aware or not, we are riding the waves of these polarities daily. One day we are praised for the job well done, the next day blamed when things go wrong. We have the experience of gain or "getting ahead" at moments of commencement, marriage, launching a new career or company, or buying a new home. The stock market rises, we are promoted, we're making money, and it seems we just might win at the game. Then something happens. Just when we thought we were getting somewhere: a cancer diagnosis, our marriage fails, we're fired, the stock market crashes, and the house is foreclosed on.

Many of us let where we are on the proverbial scorecard dictate our moods, relationships, and our entire experience of life. We move to seek pleasure and escape pain, so much so that even the slightest discomfort causes us to avoid what may be in our own best interest.

Yet these tensions can have a purpose. Imagine a relationship where one person is the passionate talker and the other is emotionally shutdown and quiet. Over time these patterns become entrenched. We get "stuck" in a rut. But the rut can have a purpose—getting our attention so that we can then use the tension effectively to grow and move forward.

Challenges Are Normal

Ask yourself this: What impact does it have on us to always approach challenges as if something is terribly wrong? How do we inadvertently increase our suffering when we act as if this is not supposed to be happening—and certainly not to me?

In Buddhist teachings, they call this the "second arrow."[39] There is the first arrow of whatever actually happens to us. Then there is the second arrow of our suffering and scarcity belief that it should not be happening *to us*. Or that it's happening to us *because* there's something wrong with us or that we are somehow bad.

Imagine what might change when you can recognize that ups and downs are normal and there's nothing wrong with you or your life. There is no single right way.

The world is always changing. Nothing on this material plane of existence lasts forever, least of all us. As one of our teachers so eloquently put it, "Until we can rest in that which does not change, we will always fear that which does."

We can learn to flow and change *with* life rather than fight the changes. Easier said than done. But, with practice, we can begin to relax into the design of this life with its dynamic tension and thrust toward evolution.

The Space between Nothing and Everything

The space at the center of the polarities is where we find the unity we crave. It's the space between the in-breath and the out-breath. It's the great unknown where all possibilities are generated and it's fertile with effortless effort and true peace. As Rumi, the Sufi poet, said so beautifully, "Out beyond ideas of wrongdoing and rightdoing, there is a field. I'll meet you there."[40] Sustainable abundance is waiting for you in that field.

Viktor Frankl, Austrian psychiatrist, author, and Holocaust survivor, states, "Between stimulus and response there is a space. In that space is our power to choose our response. In our response lies our growth and our freedom."[41]

So, *choose* to take a deeper breath; count to ten, or take a formal break in your busy day. It is in this pause that we can remind ourselves of what's okay right now. Possibilities lie within that pause. In the pause, there is rest. Gina says it this way:

> The moment in-between
> here and there
> yesterday and today
> the inhale and the exhale
> hello and goodbye
> this bite and the next
> the loving kindness and the harsh tone
> day and night

Why do we ignore the space, the silence the beauty of in-between?

How many times have we been gifted this precious space and throw it away?

Can we, in this moment, agree to accept all the moments including the spaces in-between?

Resting in the Present Moment

Remember our two simple questions from Law 2: I Am Enough—What is happening now? How is that enough? Try it here.

What is happening right now? What sensation, feeling, thought, sight, or sound are you aware of? Whatever is arising in the present is what is happening. It can evoke confusion or a sense of immediacy and enoughness.

How is that enough? It *is* enough because it *is* what is happening. Focusing on what's really happening can be the ground for great change.

It also helps us to relax to remember, "My current situation is not my permanent destination."

In the silence and stillness, a voice can be heard telling us we're okay, right now. As one of our workshop participants said, "In this law I get to rest in the lap of the divine."

Resting in a Recess from Excess

We have an opportunity in the present moment to take a recess from excess and reset. Now, as we come to understand how to live life on life's terms, it is critical we keep letting go and clearing space.

Kind of like a good cleanse or fast or any other kind of renunciation, we provide our systems with space to breathe. In that space, we can see what we need next. This is a move toward personal alignment. We exercise our right to actively participate in the choosing of what we need and what we don't. We can clean out our closets, drawers, and the underneath places in our homes, as well as the storage spaces of our minds and hearts. In this process, we often face the relationships, associations, and attachments we hold dear.

Regardless of what we hold onto, the result is that we are keeping things out of the flow of life. We can hold on to all kinds of things such as clothes, money, food, relationships, and even experiences. Sometimes we do this to escape, numb fears, or ease hurt from past experiences. It can temporarily make us feel safe and secure in an ever-changing world. But the more we hold on to that which no longer serves, the less rest we get.

The people who live in North America and Western Europe account for 12 percent of the world's population and for 60 percent of private consumption spending. We seem to be looking for safety and rest in the wrong places.

Americans spend a half a trillion dollars on nonessential items annually. Our households have more screens than people. We are drowning in things and media. Author and political commentator Van Jones says it so well: "More stuff will never heal the hole in the human heart."[42] When we relinquish something including our resentments, our anguish, or even our most precious possessions, we get a chance to rest.

Back in our Boston Sufficiency group days, we created an exercise in which we each gave something away that we held dear. First, we determined what we most did not want to let go of. Then we thought of something a bit less charged for us. Each of us found a way to let go of something we never thought we would. Some gave directly to another person they loved. Some gave to Goodwill. Whichever way we parted with the dearly held object, we learned something about holding on and letting go. And for everyone there was release. Release leads directly to rest.

Resting in Your Enough Line

When we first started exploring enough, we would access it by setting limits. If you have ever trained a dog, you have seen the power of enough in setting limits. In one simple word said in a firm and clear tone, a dog will stop what it is doing. "Enough" to the dog being trained over time comes to mean: "What you were doing was fine, but now I have had enough. So, stop." Parents may use "Enough!" similarly: "Your rowdiness, loudness, rudeness, or whining was fine for a while but now I have had enough!"

If we explore "enough," we may start to see that there is a line, of sorts, which we can trip over. When we have physically arrived at enough, sometimes we have actually gone beyond enough and into too much. We move from contentment, fun, or playfulness into annoyance, distraction, or tiredness.

We can cross the line from "enough" to "more than enough" without knowing it, and we may only find out when we notice the symptoms of excess. As you can imagine, there are "enough lines" in every domain of life.

It helps to pause and wonder: where are my enough lines? How are they drawn—thin or thick? What signals am I receiving as I approach the lines, and how do I know if I've crossed them? When we're short of a line we may be left wanting. Cross a line and we can become distressed.

Let's begin to ask ourselves some questions about our enough lines. What is enough money? What is enough time with my kids? What is enough play? What is enough rest?

We get closer to rest when we discover our enough lines and learn about our relationship to "too little," "too much," and "enough." When we have come to terms with our limitations we can breathe, relax, and let go. Asking ourselves what is enough for us and then taking the time to answer the question opens the door to satisfaction.

Stop Moving the Line

We live often in a state of chronic dissatisfaction. "If only I had more time with the kids. If only I had less stress." It's vague. Murky. And worst of all it is usually a moving target. We can get more and still we are not satisfied.

So, we ask, "What would be enough time with the kids?" And if you had it would you be willing to be satisfied? Could you rest knowing that you stood on the enough line and achieved it?

Being satisfied is a choice you make once you have declared your enough lines.

First, we define enough time with the kids: three dinners per week, one half day on weekends, being available to help with homework at least twice in a week. Okay, so now you do that. Is it enough? How would you know? We are so used to being in a state of unrest and dissatisfaction. We must train ourselves to notice, celebrate, and declare satisfaction when we do what we said we were going to do.

Otherwise, the endless chase continues. Even though we said it was enough, once we got there we moved the line a little farther. Like a colleague of ours who set a retirement number and met it years ago. Both she and her husband are still working. Once they got to the line, they moved it. "Maybe a little bit more would be better." Don't do that.

After you've done the tough work of defining your enough lines—honor them. Celebrate yourself. Declare yourself satisfied. It does not mean that things don't change and you cannot make adjustments. We aren't suggesting that. We are suggesting, however, that you use your enough lines to allow you to rest and pause.

Resting in Our Greatness: An Asset Inventory

Alan Rosenblith, our mentor about currency and the director of the film *The Money Fix*, said something we love, "We measure what we treasure and we treasure what we measure."[43]

In the scarcity story, we measure money, material assets, and accumulation of material wealth. We measure accomplishments, too, such as educational degrees and status in organizations. In a world of sustainable abundance there is so much more worth measuring. The good news is you get to declare what it is you treasure. The number of conversations you have with your adult son, how many days you snow ski in April, counting the states or countries you have visited, even the number of diapers you get to change. When we expand our definition of what we treasure, and what is worthy of measuring, our view of what is valuable expands.

If we have a gratitude practice, we may already appreciate the power of acknowledging the best parts of situations, others, and ourselves. Putting our attention on what is working already can shift a mood, a perspective, or a process and can help unstick any psychic or emotional congestion we may be feeling. In focusing on getting ahead or on not lagging behind, we often forget to acknowledge the vast web of resources beyond money that support us and help us rest.

Let us take stock of our nonmonetary or intangible assets. Often when we do an asset inventory we can discover sources of support we were not yet aware of, parts of our life we had not yet appreciated, or refine our enough line. Regardless of how vast or limited our material wealth may be, we have a deep well of resources to pull from when we conduct our inventory.

Looking at our assets in this expanded way is not only refreshing, it is a clear way through scarcity thinking, delivering us right into the arms of what is enough. Attending to what is already working and what you already have immediately shifts you.

Jen has a dear friend who lives in a beautiful mountain town. She has never made much money. She has *always* had enough, though it hasn't always felt that way. She has little savings and by today's standards would be considered underresourced for her "retirement." When using the measurements of our scarcity-driven culture, she has less than enough.

But she lives in a beautiful mountain town. Her three children have all moved back to their hometown to be near her. Her children have already said they will make sure she is cared for. She has a community of people in whom she has invested for over thirty years. She has a partner with whom she has done the work of building a working relationship filled with respect and kindness. It's a different kind of currency she can count on when the chips are down.

When she factors all of that into her asset inventory, she's wealthy in the ways that matter to her. These are some of the currencies of sustainable abundance, and she chose them consciously and carefully.

practices
for law 5

Practice #1:
My "Enough Line"

- Where is my enough line? (Often it is different in different domains of our lives, so we invite you to distinguish it in as many ways as you can. Look at money, love, time with children, success, square footage, enlightenment, workshops, friendships, clothing, cars, homes, food.)
- What happens to me physically, emotionally, and spiritually when I have more than enough?
- When have I ever gotten less than enough? What emotions arise and what happens physically?
- Am I willing to accept what I thought was less than enough?

Practice #2:
Taking My Asset Inventory

Settle into a quiet space. Take a few deep centering breaths and exhale out any tension. If you like to write, get your journal and put it next to you. We will offer a series of questions. Take a minute or so between each question and write your responses as a free flow stream of consciousness, whatever arises.

Use any format that works for you. If you like to write lists, write a list, or if you want to write a story, write a story. Notice too if there is any resistance, or if there are any negative predictions, or old narratives.

- What are you grateful for? You can be grateful for anything. Now or in the past, even something you're looking forward to.
- What do you appreciate about yourself? Right now, in this moment, and in the past.
- What character attributes and capabilities do you rely on?
- What accomplishments are you proud of?
- Who can you count on?
- What are you good at?
- What do you love to do?
- How do you like to spend your time?
- What brings you joy?
- What brings you laughter?
- What's fun for you?
- What's working in your relationships with your immediate family, your extended family, your colleagues, people at school or church, and the grocery store?
- What do you love about your work in the world: about your home, about your work, inside the house, outside the house, volunteer work, paid work?
- If you have children, what do you love about them?
- What do you love about your friends? If a companion or a best friend stands out, what do you love about that person?

- If you have a partner or significant other, what do you love about them?
- If you have animals, what do you love about them?
- What do you love about your family?
- What daily rituals nourish you?
- What are your actions, or ways of being or steps you take, things that mark your day?

Have a look at this list in total now. These are the assets you have in your life that we sometimes do not measure or simply overlook. What begins to open for you when you count more than just money in your treasure trove of resources?

FEEL THE RESISTANCE

You've just spent time investigating the assets you already have available to you. Take a moment now and notice if there is any resistance. Oftentimes when we spend time valuing ourselves as sustainable and abundant, the monsters of scarcity rise back up to greet us.

You might start hearing that voice, "But I don't have enough of this or that." Notice if there is any rebellion against your own sufficiency and simply allow it to be there. Know that this is natural.

Take three or four deep breaths right now. See if you can allow the container of your own body to be expansive enough, malleable enough to hold and make room for all that already is. Everything you have, everything you are already good at. Everything you appreciate about yourself right now. Everyone in your life that you can count on that you love. Every single external and internal resource available to you right now. See if you can make room and receive all that you have and all that you are.

Practice #3:

Mindfulness of Feelings/Body Scan

When we engage in our mindfulness practice, we begin to observe that each sensation, emotion, or thought has a "feeling tone" that goes with it (see the practices section of Law 2). This may not be obvious at first but with practice we can observe that everything we sense, feel, or think is either pleasant, unpleasant, or neutral to the mind. We note, for example, "tingling" or "piercing" and then ask ourselves is this sensation pleasant, unpleasant, or neutral? Let's practice:

Take a moment to pause. Feel the touch of your breath and once you are settled, begin to scan your body starting with the bottoms of the feet.

Note whether your thoughts, sensations, or emotions are pleasant, unpleasant, or neutral. Notice what causes unpleasant experiences to arise and what causes them to stop.

Similarly do that for pleasant experiences and neutral ones.

You are noting the *feeling tones* of what's happening within you and nothing else.

Now let your awareness move slowly upward through the body. Move into the lower legs (you may want to focus your attention on one foot and leg and then the other) noticing sensation, feeling, thought, and noting feeling tone.

Keep bringing your awareness upward and move into the torso, pausing to notice what is arising and then note the feeling tone that corresponds with what is arising.

Continue upward through the trunk of the body into the chest and chest area.

Then bring your awareness to your fingertips in your right hand and scan up the right arm and then do the same on the left side, all the while noting the feeling tones.

Bring your attention to the back of the shoulders where each arm connects and continue bringing your awareness to the neck and into the head, finally resting the attention at the crown and noting what is arising along with the feeling tone.

You may do another sweep through the body or stop and relax back into breath here. As we cultivate an awareness of feeling tones in the moment, we can unwind and rest in ourselves regardless of our circumstance.

Practice #4:
The Tools of Sufficiency

Whenever you notice a weapon of scarcity in play, choose a tool of sufficiency to use in the moment and remind you that you are enough.

For example, if you feel fear during the day, choose the tool "what is" and ground yourself in the moment. This could happen many times in a day. Experiment with this process and notice your relationship to scarcity at the end of the day.

Practice #5:
Lie on the Floor

At the end of our first year in business, we prepared our first strategy session. One of our board members said he wanted us to let that all go and just lie on the floor at the retreat center.

We were flabbergasted and a little incredulous—we wanted to be taken seriously. We were building a business, not launching a hobby. But we were also committed to our own growth and development so we honored their request.

We lay on the floor, sat in comfortable chairs, reclined on couches, went for walks—and never took out our agenda. The funny thing was that at the end of the retreat we had covered all the agenda items and had a plan for the future of the business. At the same time, we were rested and nourished and our partnership renewed.

Where can you let go of plans and experiment with your own "lie on the floor" protocol?

Practice #6:
Making Space

Literally, make space in your life. What can you let go of materially? Make a move now or put time in your calendar to practice releasing anything that does not bring you joy and ease. Invite a friend to join you and then go to their house and return the favor.

- Empty your junk drawer(s).
- Look in your closet and drawers and release anything that you haven't worn this year.
- Empty any box you haven't opened since you last moved.
- Give something away each day for thirty days.
- Don't go grocery shopping until you have eaten or given away all the food in your pantry.

- Clean your attic, basement, or garage this month.
- Empty your storage facility and take six months of the monthly expense and gift it to a friend or invest it in an organization that is aligned with your personal mission and values.

Practice #7:
Finding Your "Sustaining Book"

This experiment allows us to learn from the wisdom of A. A. Milne, the author of *Winnie the Pooh*. After reading to her son one evening, Gina wrote the following:

> "Great Tightness" was the phrase that caught my attention first. That's what scarcity feels like to me. Am I "Wedged in a Great Tightness" like Winnie-the-Pooh was wedged in Rabbit's door? All Pooh had to do to get free was wait a week—don't eat and then have his community push him out.
>
> This feels comforting to me. When I feel a "Great Tightness" maybe I just need to sit and wait and then have my friends give me the extra support I need to break free.
>
> In *Winnie the Pooh*, the sustaining book is an alphabet picture book that Christopher Robin reads to Pooh. The illustration shows Christopher Robin has paused at the letter J for JAM. I assume that since Pooh couldn't eat honey or jam for the week Christopher Robin thought that reading to him about jam would make him feel better for not having any.

What could your sustaining book be? What would nourish and sustain you in the moment?

Take the time to write your own sustaining book. You might want to follow the alphabet like in *Winnie-the-Pooh*. If you have more time, you could write a short booklet that you could rest in when things don't seem all right. Below is an example of one Gina wrote.

GINA'S SUSTAINING BOOK, SUCH AS WOULD HELP AND COMFORT A WEDGED PERSON IN A GREAT TIGHTNESS:

A Art	J Joy	S Smiles
B Biking	K Kites	T Truth
C Courage	L Love	U Unconditional
D Dog	M Mud	V Veggies
E Enough	N Nourishment	W Wonder
F Flow	O Open	X "X-ing x's"
G Goodness	P Possible	Y Yes
H Holding Hands	Q Quiet	Z Zipper
I Inquiry	R Rain	

law 6
joy is
available

How does joy live in me?

Humor, laughter, and a lightness of being are natural results of accepting what is already here. These are gateways to joy and once we learn to let go and sink into something truly embracing, the heart begins to feel buoyant. There's a famous *New Yorker* cartoon, by Bob Mankoff, in which we see a man on the phone saying, "No, Thursday's out.

How about never—is never good for you?" that cuts to the heart of this law. We can find a way to laugh about the hard stuff and see that it doesn't have to be all that serious after all.

Laughter and Forgiveness

When Jen was younger, nothing seemed funny. Everything was serious—even critical. It was never "all right" and there was no rest for the weary—always too much work to be done. Serious work—the work to end suffering! We know it sounds dramatic, but that's how it felt at the time. Jen's inability to laugh at herself, or at much of anything at all, pointed to a deeper skill set that was missing: the ability to forgive—forgive herself and the world for not being perfect. "If you can laugh at yourself, you can forgive yourself," Susan Sparks, author of *Laugh Your Way to Grace: Reclaiming the Spiritual Power of Humor*, writes in a *Psychology Today* blog. "And if you can forgive yourself, you can forgive others."

That was not yet in Jen's repertoire. It would take time and lots of practice of everything we have been talking about so far. In order for life to have meaning, she committed to take on the creation of a world where everyone and everything mattered.

It's not that she *never* laughed, but it was rare. And when others could, and did, especially about serious things, she was mortified, angry, offended. In 2001 Jen hired a coach to support her in her business. This was before she met Gina and started Seven Stones. The coach asked, "What would it take for you to be delighted with your work?" Jen could barely say the word "delighted." Satisfied, maybe. Being delighted seemed wrong, almost trivial in the face of her suffering and the suffering of others.

That was the year of 9/11 after all. Laughter? Delight? Viktor Frankl states, "It is well known that humor, more than anything else in the human makeup, can afford an aloofness and an ability to rise above any situation, even if only for a few seconds."[44]

Over the years, and we do mean years, delight became available. Now Jen laughs at herself and people tell her she's funny. Her lightness of being is an outgrowth of practicing literally *all* of the practices we have offered so far.

As she claimed her belonging and her enoughness, her sense of rest and ease increased. Then she noticed it was easier to laugh at herself, and even the hard stuff. Forgiveness became available both for herself, for life as it is, and for others. Joy and lightness followed.

She still has never been more dedicated to the alleviation of suffering. However, now there is balance, and a genuine joy that emerges spontaneously even in the face of her suffering and others'.

A teacher of ours used to always say, "Death is on your side." As we get closer to facing the truth that we are not exempt from any of life's tragedies and triumphs, we soften. We loosen our grip. When we let go, we make way for joy and humor to enter.

Knowing that we are not exempt (Law 4) and that we are going to die can be heavy! So we say "Lighten up." Rabbi Earl A. Grollman writes, "While death, dying, and loss are no laughing matter, those who find a bit of humor in the grieving process know that they will survive."[45]

Jack Kornfield, Buddhist teacher and scholar, told a story while Jen was on retreat. It was about a famous South American golfer. After winning a tournament and receiving his check, he was approached in the parking lot by a young woman. She told him she had a child who was ill and probably going to die. De Vincenzo, the golfer, took out a pen and turned over his winnings to the young woman. A week or so later De Vincenzo was in the clubhouse with friends. An official came over to the table to let him know that the woman in the parking lot was a fraud. She had no sick baby.

"You mean there is no baby who is dying?" De Vincenzo asked.

"That's right," the official said. "You have been fleeced."

"That is the best news I have heard all week."

Laughing at Ourselves

In some ways our laughing at ourselves, our foibles and eccentricities, is a reminder that *we will make it . . . until we don't.* The ability to be self-deprecating and rest in humor is a way of letting go. We can let go of our significance and self-importance, be comfortable with our foot in our mouth, our clumsiness and with our failures.

The passing of time is often useful here. It offers us perspective and an ability to bring compassion and lightness to something that previously felt so heavy and serious. Being able to see irony and paradox in ourselves as we travel through life provides a buffer for the many vicissitudes we all encounter.

Humor and comedy can also be a way for us to heal a collective wound and to talk about the things that matter most. It's an important way to counteract and overcome fear, address social issues like inequality, and to understand the larger world.

After 9/11, many of us tuned in to David Letterman as he returned on air on September seventeenth. We wondered how he could entertain us in a world broken by such horror. What was clear was he just needed to *be* with us. He could, and did, remind us that we knew how to laugh. What's more, our laughter was a sign that we, as a nation and as individuals, could and would begin to move forward out of our shock and grief.

Humor as a Weapon or Shield

Yes, we can use humor constructively to defuse tense situations and even get out of trouble. But, as with many positive things, humor can also be used as a weapon and block joy from arising. In fear or scarcity, we can use humor to make fun of others, to belittle them or make ourselves seem superior. Humor can also be used to humiliate and shun people. Jokes can be used dangerously by one group to make another seem inferior or even support horrible stereotypes. Mocking humor can be misused to lessen our sense of empathy toward others by making them the butt of our jokes.

Discovering joy through the process of lightening up is different from telling someone to "lighten up!" We might think we're doing that jokingly, but it's really aggressive and dismissive. When anger arises for someone, they usually want to be seen and heard. It's not a moment to tell them to lighten up, and when we do, it's often to soothe ourselves. Maybe their anger scares us. Thoughtlessly telling someone to "lighten up" only stops the flow of whatever is happening, including joy.

The same is true of telling the other person they're "overreacting" or are "too sensitive." This often happens to people in oppressed groups. They get told to squelch their complaints of injustice. If only "they" could lighten up and be less sensitive and take it all less seriously then "we" would be free to turn away from the very real suffering in front of us.

We often use "nervous laughter" as a kind of unconscious shield. It's an expression of tension and anxiety or discomfort, but unlike joyful laughter, it doesn't relax you, it can make you, and the people around you, more nervous.

Self-deprecating humor can be used both as a shield, and as a weapon against ourselves. Why wait for someone to make fun of us, when we can make a joke at our own expense? While this can be a positive form of laughing at yourself, it can also be self-critical and belittling.

Humor for Well-Being

In the Dalai Lama's book *My Spiritual Journey*, he says, "I have been confronted with many difficulties throughout the course of my life, and my country is going through a critical period. But I laugh often, and my laughter is contagious. When people ask me how I find the strength to laugh now, I reply that I am a professional laugher."[46]

Humor is medicinal, a potent remedy that heals us. We see something funny and we laugh. That laughter has many benefits. According to Dr. Lee Berk and Dr. Stanley Tan at Loma Linda University, the anticipation of laughter reduces stress hormones, improves good cholesterol, boosts T cells, triggers the release of endorphins, and produces an overall sense of well-being.[47]

Norman Cousins, an American political journalist, author, professor, and world peace advocate, was told he was going to die within four months. In his book *Anatomy of an Illness as Perceived by the Patient: Reflections on Healing and Regeneration*, he wrote, "I made the joyous discovery that ten minutes of genuine belly laughter had an anesthetic effect and would give me at least two hours of pain-free sleep."[48] Funny movies were medicine that worked. Doctors only gave him a one in five hundred chance of recovery, yet he did, and lived twenty-six more years.

Laughter's effects have been studied and documented. Both dopamine and epinephrine levels decrease after exposure to humor and laughter. Humor helps our immune system stay strong or get stronger. In the wake of these studies, both laughter clubs and laughter yoga have emerged as avenues for relieving stress, increasing joy, and building connections in groups and even working teams.

It is easy to try humor as medicine. The next time you are down or feel melancholy, pick up a funny book, turn on your favorite comedy, watch your favorite comic on stage, or go to YouTube to watch the clips that make you laugh. Give yourself an opportunity to laugh and guffaw out loud if possible, note your mood before you laughed and after; notice what shifts. Our ability to make fun of any situation, to bring lightness to any circumstance can make a difference. Maurice Vanderpol, a former president of the Boston Psychoanalytic Society and Institute, reports in *Harvard Business Review* that, "Survivors of concentration camps had what he calls a 'plastic shield.' The shield was comprised of several factors, including a sense of humor. Often the humor was [macabre], but nonetheless it provided a critical sense of perspective."[49]

When we swim in the sea of scarcity we lose perspective. In 1835 Alexis de Tocqueville stated in his treatise *Democracy in America*, "In America I saw the freest and most enlightened men placed in the happiest condition that exists in the world; it seemed to me that a sort of cloud habitually covered their features; they appeared to me grave and almost sad even in their pleasures."[50] In mid-seventeenth-century America, we were already actively playing the great accumulation game of *more is better* and over the past 150 years we have taken the game to new heights. Our false belief that our possessions bring us joy and happiness has left us lost and unable to find our way.

In *The Book of Joy*, Douglas Abrams, who spent time with both Archbishop Desmond Tutu and His Holiness the Dalai Lama, reports, "They and everyone around them were constantly guffawing, chortling, giggling, and belly laughing throughout the week, as moments of great levity were spliced together with moments of profundity and sanctity. So often their first response to any subject, no matter how seemingly painful, was to laugh."[51] Both these men have endured and seen great suffering. Both have been spiritual leaders for nations torn apart by racism, war, hatred, and great acts of violence against their people and even against themselves. Yet they laugh.

This laughter became available through years of cultivating a presence of heart and mind. In the same book, the Dalai Lama outlines eight pillars of a life of joy. He spoke about perspective, humility, humor, and acceptance as qualities of mind to be cultivated for joy to arise naturally. And how cultivating forgiveness, gratitude, compassion, and generosity will lead to joy in the heart.

Humor and Joy: A Partnership

Jack Kornfield writes, "There is deep joy that arises when we stop denying the painful aspects of life, and instead allow our hearts to open to and accept the full range of human experience: life and death, pleasure and pain, darkness and light. Even in the face of the tremendous suffering in the world, there can be joy, which comes not from rejecting pain and seeking pleasure but rather from our ability to . . . open ourselves to the truth."[52]

Joy can be the companion or the foundation of any circumstance, wonderful or challenging. Joy is light shining and reflecting from our hearts. It is the expression of awe and wonder. Do you know someone who can access the pleasure of being alive even when they are scared, worried, or confronted?

"The present moment is filled with joy and happiness. If you are attentive, you will see it," writes Thich Nhat Hanh, a Buddhist monk, writer, and activist. "When we are mindful, deeply in touch with the present moment, our understanding of what is going on deepens, and we begin to be filled with acceptance, joy, peace, and love."[53]

Again, from *The Book of Joy*, Desmond Tutu states, "Discovering more joy does not, I'm sorry to say, save us from the inevitability of hardship and heartbreak. In fact, we may cry more easily, but we will laugh more easily, too. Perhaps we are just more alive. Yes, as we discover more joy, we can face suffering in a way that ennobles rather than embitters. We have hardship without becoming hard. We have heartbreak without becoming broken."[54]

From a state of joy, we recognize our enoughness with ease. Bringing joy, celebration, and passion to our lives and our work is another way to generate sustainable abundance. It helps us celebrate small wins, and be positive, grateful, and content with life.

Looking for places to insert a lightness of being into our lives brings an effervescent quality to our daily experience.

Until five years ago Gina didn't even realize that joy was elusive to her. She discovered this while testing a phone app for a friend of hers. The app pinged her at various times of the day and asked a series of questions. One was about joy. Gina noticed she was never feeling joy when prompted. This led her to investigate her relationship to joy and actively cultivate it.

Jen also noticed that her experience of joy was difficult to feel in an ongoing way. She would often have access to it for moments, yet recalled having only two long-lasting experiences of joy. "When I experienced it, I felt a sense of well-being and enoughness that was quite something. There was this store I loved, and it had been the source of much longing and envy over the years when I couldn't afford to shop there. Plagued by comparison, one of the weapons of scarcity, I had spent a lot of time wondering why other people got so lucky as to be able to buy lovely things there. But now, in this prolonged mood of joy and deep contentment, I had this sense I needed or wanted nothing. The store had no appeal. It was not me saying to myself, 'You don't need anything. You are fine. Just keep walking.' It was me not having a sense of interest in anything outside of the deep well of joy that was present. It was truly striking, a moment in sharp contrast to my usual internal state." In this state, there is joy in just being alive. There's no need to add more.

Sympathetic Joy

There is a way to magnify our joy. Buddhist teachings call it "sympathetic joy." It's the practice of experiencing joy at someone else's happiness. In the story of scarcity, we often feel envy or jealousy at another's good fortune, especially in the face of our misery. In a state of sympathetic joy, we know there is enough to go around.

Your good fortune does not rob me of my potential good fortune today or in the future. Rather, it's an opportunity to magnify joy because I cannot only feel it for myself, but equally for others. Your success allows for my heart to expand and for me to take pleasure in all of life.

Both of us have found an unexpected outcome from lightening up, laughing, relaxing, and enjoying life. We have recovered our creative selves. Jen started singing again, like she did as a child. Now she sings in her yearly community play and at some of our workshops.

Gina started making collages and encourages our clients to make her simple three-image collage as a practice to weave joy and humor into their lives. Our recovered creative expression arose naturally. We believe that the lightness of being that arises from humor and joy is deeply intertwined with our ability to develop unconditional love, our final and possibly ultimate sign-post of enough.

practices
for law 6

Practice #1:
Gina's Practice for Cultivating Joy

To explicitly cultivate joy, Gina does the following journal practice before heading to bed. Start this practice with a thirty-day commitment. Write something about each of these topics:

- *What am I grateful for?* This is a way to remember the special or forgotten moments of the day.
- *What am I proud of?* This question helps you focus and bring your attention to your inherent goodness.
- *What am I longing for?* To tap into longing helps you feel your fragility and brings your awareness to the preciousness of life.

Practice #2:
Joy Inventory

- What small wins can I celebrate in this moment?
- What aspects of my work and career are fun and fuel my passion?
- Where am I positive, grateful, and content with life?
- When today did I feel content or even happy for no reason?
- When was the last time I experienced a sense of awe?

Practice #3:

Feeling Checkup

Set an alarm to go off six times over the course of the day. When you hear the alarm, pause and take the time to make note of what you were doing; then notice your feelings. Where did you fall along this spectrum: relaxed, anxious, joyful, tired, content, sad, excited, irritable?

Jot down your feelings throughout the day. After a week of experimenting, see what patterns arise.

Also, can you pinpoint what actions and time of day cause different feeling tones? Finally, notice, in particular, the causes of joy.

Practice #4:

Gina's Three-Image Collage

We have found making collages a great way to explore, investigate, and cultivate joy. It's useful when you're feeling confused, stuck, or are just taking yourself too seriously. Making a collage is not only fun, it can be revealing, letting your unconscious send you messages, as if in a dream. You can make them with regular household items.

Gather your supplies:

- Magazines, newspapers, or computer images (Google Images and Pinterest are great online resources).
- Glue, staple, or tape.
- Scissors.
- Old manila folders, cardboard, card stock paper, or your journal.

The key is to trust your initial attraction or repulsion to an image.

Quickly skim, or glance over, images and make selections, ripping or cutting them out.

Once you gather at least three images and no more than ten, start to glue, staple, or tape them to a piece of paper in your journal, on a note-pad, the manila folder, or other surface. You can also create one online if you have a graphics program.

HELPFUL HINTS:

- Spend no more than thirty minutes on a collage. (Fifteen min-utes is recommended.)
- There is no need to spend time thinking about the images or how they fit together. Just go with your gut.

Here are some questions to consider about your collage. You may want to put your final collage aside for twenty-four hours and then look at it again.

- What do you notice?
- What surprised you about the collage itself or your process?
- What insights do you have after this exercise?
- Is there anything to share with the people in your life?

Practice #5:
One-Minute Laughter

Laugh every day for a week, set your timer for one minute and laugh out loud. Make sure you include different types of laughs over the course of your practice including:

- Giggling
- Cackle

- Chortle
- High-pitched laugh
- Santa laugh
- Hee-haw laugh
- Belly laugh

This is a great practice to do with your family and friends. Alert: you may find that you are laughing for longer than a minute.

Practice #6:
Movie Time

Watch AFI's 100 Greatest American Movie Comedies of All Time or IMDB's 100 All-Time Greatest Comedy Films or ask your ten best friends what is their number-one comedy film and watch them, too. Here are a few films to get you started:

- *Groundhog Day*
- *Annie Hall*
- *Bridesmaids*
- *Monty Python and the Holy Grail*
- *Airplane!*
- *Blazing Saddles*
- *Trainwreck*

law 7
love is the answer

How well did I love myself today?

Love is the answer is the seventh and final law of enough. Living the six previous laws has strengthened our mind-heart connection to prepare us for an unconditional acceptance of love. The mind-set of enough allows us to choose to love generously, without reserve, and *without the expectation of getting something in return.*

We often forget that love is not limited to the feeling of attraction. Love is a discipline, a practice, a conferring of trust before it is earned. Love is being there when it's inconvenient, uncomfortable, and when you are not in the mood. It's the recognition and acceptance of everyone's enoughness, regardless of the circumstances.

In the context of sustainable abundance, it becomes possible to drop love as quid pro quo. This is the essential point of living in the mind-set of enough. In Sharon Salzberg's book *Loving-Kindness: The Revolutionary Art of Happiness*, she writes, "Fear is the primary mechanism sustaining the concept of 'the other' and reinforcing the subsequent loneliness and distance in our lives. Ranging from numbness to terror, fear constricts our hearts and binds us to a false and misleading way of viewing life. That fallacy of separate existence cloaks itself in the beguiling forms of our identifications. We identify with a fragment of reality rather than with the whole."

Love in the Context of Scarcity

Love is a loaded word. Instead of being an expansive way to relate to the world, it's sold as a confining cliché where one-size-supposedly-fits-all.

We see the standard, heterosexual "love story" repeated, endlessly: *Snow White. Cinderella. Sleeping Beauty. Little Mermaid. Beauty and the Beast. Pretty Woman.* A woman/beautiful princess falls for a man/charming prince, she has to be saved by him, and they live happily ever after.

The moral: we must find our one true love and get married and live happily ever after. If we fail, there's something wrong with us.

Love, thankfully, is deeper and more nuanced than that. In this context, "love" is not intended to mean romantic love, but the very energetic fabric of the universe. It is the fiber of all connections; it is the integral ingredient that makes everything work. Love is limitless, and enduring. We humans express love through our very attention; we direct it with our words and actions. We come into knowing love by nourishing it. People, places, and things are the conduits of love and so we have the experience of loving *something*. But love itself is the light, the energy, the directed attention itself, and loving is a practice.

In *The Law of Love*, Mahatma Gandhi wrote, "Whether mankind will consciously follow the law of love, I do not know. But that need not perturb us. The law will work, just as the law of gravitation will work, whether we accept it or not. Just as a scientist will work wonders out of various applications of the law of nature, even so a man who applies the law of love with scientific precision can work greater wonders."[55]

When we "fall in love," we feel all kinds of feelings. The brain lights up in the same areas as when we are addicted to something. It's part of how we create a pair bond. And, like addiction, once that feeling dies down, we want *more*.

But this can lead us to think love is something to give and get, to feel, to claim, to dole out sparingly lest we get hurt. If our love fades away, it seems we have no power in the face of our changing experience, so we go our separate ways. Sometimes we manage to maintain a modicum of dignity in the separating. Sometimes we produce great harm and cause suffering as we separate bodies, hearts, and belongings, and reconfigure the design of the family.

The word "love" itself is deemed suitable for certain contexts, downright inappropriate in others. We tend not to say, "I love you" to the letter carrier, the gas station attendant, or the cashier. We certainly do not talk about love in the modern workplace. At work, we are allowed to care, even to have a passionate vision that includes being good to people and even the planet. But love? Fear and scarcity drive the modern workplace. Not love.

We reserve our love for the special connections we have in our lives. The children we raise, or the people we have declared our love for. For everyone else, we may like or care for them, or are possibly indifferent to them, or even dislike or hate them. However, there is no love. This is all part of the paradigm of separation. Some people are part of our tribe and deserve our attention. Others, not so much, or not at all. We think we're keeping ourselves protected with our us-versus-them, either/or, me-versus-you beliefs. What we are doing instead is living the scarcity story.

As a young woman, Jen was angry much of the time and filled with despair about our world. She was righteous and thought she had the "right" answers to pretty much everything. Loving the good guys and hating the bad guys seemed just fine to her. The fire of righteous rage was burning her up as much as it was fueling anything good.

Still she thought that her hatred of "them" was not bad. She *knew* she was on the right side of the argument, which meant it was okay to be furious and hate the enemy. Her philosophy at the time was, "If you're not outraged, you're not paying attention." She was paying very close attention to the systems of oppression and to the larger contexts and stories pressing on everyone. Dramatic, but that's how she felt.

In 1993, Jen did a yearlong training. Each person had to write their life story. No matter their gender, racial background, sexuality, or age, everybody had a story. Remember Law 1. No matter how different they appeared to her or how separate she felt from them initially, hearing their life stories dramatically changed how she saw them.

"They" were suddenly just like her. They, too, had hopes and dreams, fears and sorrows. They had hardships and faced pain just like her—regardless of their age, gender, race, or anything else she'd previously categorized as other. *They* stopped being separate or different.

"I am" became "we are." As that false dichotomy began to crumble, Jen began to question rage as a force for transformation and change. She thought, "I am just like them, only I think I'm right. Maybe there's no such thing as *them*. Maybe there's only *we* with different histories, stories, ideas, and views."

She started to feel how love and compassion could provide another way. And, maybe, she could get relief from the burning rage eating away at her heart. This realization would change how she saw everything and lead directly to the world of enough.

Cultivating Love

How do we put ourselves in a state of love? We call it forth, invite it, invoke it. We bring it into being through our words, our somatic shaping, and our commitments. Our tools include the following:

- understanding
- trust
- acceptance

- compassion
- the capacity to let go of anger
- and the ability to see all people's essential nature

As we cultivate these capacities, our basic feelings of love for all beings can grow. What if love was seeing ourselves and others clearly—and accepting them fully for who they truly are and are not? What if we extended our sight to love *all* children, *all* women, and *all* men regardless of where they live, what they look like, or if we have or will ever meet them? We can extend our love to all animals, living things, and the biosphere.

What Is Love?

Love is a verb, a place to stand, a choice, a call from deep within. Our anatomy and physiology are designed for it. Love is letting go of how we thought it was supposed to be. Love is seeing yourself and another clearly. Love is knowing what you hold most dear and being willing to fight for it. Love is the welling up of gratitude that comes when you feel yourself truly connected to all beings. Love is someone standing for you when you don't know how to stand for yourself. Love is acceptance—the ability to be with it all: the parts we like, the parts we hate, the parts we wish would just disappear. Love is finding out that none of it deserves to be discarded, that it all has a place, that all of it belongs, that all of you belongs. Love is having the courage to forgive those who will harm you. It is a willingness to see their humanness, their frailty, their fear, and to choose not to condemn them for it. Love is being able to forgive all your failings and to grant them equal space at the table with your greatest successes.

Love is a beckoning voice, calling you deeply to yourself, deeply to your truth, to your path, to your own dance between nothing and everything, to the creation that will be your life.

What is *your* definition of love?

What if we offered our love freely, generously, and fully? What kind of world would that make? When we choose love in any moment where scarcity is lurking, we transform it. Aleksandr Solzhenitsyn, the Russian author, said, "If only it were so simple. If only there were evil people somewhere insidiously committing evil deeds, and it were necessary just to separate them from the rest of us and destroy them. But the line dividing good and evil cuts through the heart of every human being. And who among us is willing to destroy a piece of their own heart."[56]

Love is simple but not easy. Loving can feel dangerous because it opens us to vulnerability and hurt. Yet when we return to love as a disciplined practice, every day, we remember, I am enough, I have enough.

Daring to Love Yourself

Sharon Salzberg shared a story about attending a conference in Dharamsala, India, with the Dalai Lama. This conference had Indian philosophers, psychologists, scientists, as well as practitioners from Western countries in attendance. Sharon got the opportunity to ask a question that was foremost on her mind, "What do you think about self-hatred?"

> The room went quiet as all of us awaited the answer of the Dalai Lama, revered leader of Tibetan Buddhism. Looking startled, he turned to his translator and asked pointedly in Tibetan again

and again for an explanation. Finally, turning back to me, the Dalai Lama tilted his head, his eyes narrowed in confusion. 'Self-hatred?' he repeated in English. 'What is that?' For the Western meditation teachers in the room and for us today it feels inconceivable to have a mind that does not know what it means to hate the self. Salzberg continues, During the remainder of the session, the Dalai Lama repeatedly attempted to explore the contours of self-hatred with us. At the end he said, "I thought I had a very good acquaintance with the mind, but now I feel quite ignorant. I find this very, very strange."[57]

We say that self-loathing is a weapon of scarcity. Tara Brach, psychologist, author, and teacher of meditation agrees. She has stated that the most endemic disease in the West is not diabetes or obesity, it's self-loathing.[58] Why is self-loving so complicated and fraught with fear?

Hopefully by now we can see how a culture of scarcity both undermines the self and demands a kind of endless betterment of this flawed package. Michele McDonald, a meditation teacher, told a story about a young Western monk she met in Burma. He was radiant and clearly truly happy. She asked him one day, "How did you do it, get this happy?" He looked at her and reported back, "It took me nine years to work through my self-loathing."[59]

As she heard the story, Jen recalls not quite knowing if this was the good news or the bad. Here he was on duty 24/7 practicing to let go of self-hatred and it took *nine years*! How on earth would any layperson have any hope of achieving that kind of quiet inner peace in a lifetime?

Jen realized it was both good and bad news. With effort, trained attention, and practice we can liberate the heart and mind from the conditioning of scarcity. That said, the scarcity story is so deep. And we well know, human beings make mistakes, fall as much as we walk, at least for a time, forget and then remember.

After all of that, what can we find left to love? In the context of enough, there is plenty. It includes our foibles, our shadow, our exiled parts, and our wrinkled skin. The self-loathing fades as we find a way to become a friend to the "self."

Part of why we wrote this book is to give us all an opportunity to experience ease and friendliness toward this very precious being we call "me." We can have this opportunity each day when we ask ourselves, "How well did I love myself today?"

Love in Action

Gina lived in a cottage in Cambridge, Massachusetts. Behind her property was a storage facility that took up a city block. One day, she and all her neighbors got a postcard letting them know that a developer had made an offer to buy the storage facility to develop homes. They were invited to a community meeting to hear about it. When they arrived at the meeting they came to discover the developer wanted to build 127 condominiums on a three-acre parcel of land.

The attitude of the developer and landowner was that we should be overjoyed and happy to have this large construction project come to the neighborhood because it could raise our property values. But the land was bound by two narrow busy thoroughfares, which were already highly congested, and the developers had made no plans for parking. And when the homeowners looked at the height and size of the buildings in comparison to their small cottages, it was clear the new development would dwarf them.

All of this was legal inside of Cambridge's zoning ordinance, yet, in the end, no development happened. How did the neighbors stop it? By taking a stand from love rather than fighting. They began talking and, for the first time, discovered each other as people. They learned about each other's skills, as well as their combined weaknesses and strengths. They learned zoning law and the process for planning and building. They created a new name for their neighborhood—to define themselves rather than let the developer and landowner define them. They used the available technology to coalesce the neighborhood and host community meetings.

They didn't talk about stopping the development or about not wanting people to come into the neighborhood. Instead, they discussed their vision for their neighborhood, how they loved it, and why people would want to come and live there.

They worked together as a community. They talked to their city councilors and went to the planning board, only to have their petition rejected by the city. They persevered and discovered that there were commercial properties and business owners that would be negatively impacted by their petition to stop the development. Instead of seeing them as enemies, they struck a compromise with them. Before that moment, neither party considered themselves to be part of the neighborhood. Now they had created a more inclusive, and stronger, community and coalition.

With a larger community and more support, the city council unanimously voted to support the new plan. They weren't hostile, nor did they condemn the developer. They simply stood in love and inclusion for all. This is love in action.

If you are a community organizer, go organize your community to effect change that you most care about. If you are a fundraiser, go raise funds to fund the future that calls you forth.

STANDING FOR RATHER THAN AGAINST

Inside sustainable abundance we can stand *for* rather than fight *against*. As a peaceful warrior we believe all things are possible. Lynne Twist states, "Great leaders know the distinction between taking a position and taking a stand. Taking a stand creates a field where all positions are heard and respected and truth begins to have room to be expressed."[60]

A PATHWAY TO LOVE IN ACTION

Here's the path Gina and her neighbors followed to stand for what they wanted to see happen in their neighborhood.

Pause   This is where we choose to take action. Pausing helps us gather our energies and move consciously.

Inquire   Be curious and interested. Let go of assumptions. Show up with openness.

Gather   A community where we can rest and join into a stronger resource.

Let Go   We remember we'll have to let go of everything eventually. Letting go makes room for multiple ways of seeing. It allows us to include as much as we can. This helps us move from positions to interests.

Stand   Honing commitment and a bridge to the future.

Committed Action   Taking the next right step, repeatedly, from loving awareness. Making room to go through all of the above stages again and again throughout the process.

Love and Courage

Choosing love, in word and deed, takes courage. We must face our fears to love anything in life, whether in intimate relationships or the larger world.

In her book *Conscience and Courage: Rescuers of Jews during the Holocaust,* Eva Fogelman tells the story of Marion van Binsbergen Pritchard, a social work student.[61] It was 1942 and she was riding her bike past a Jewish children's home. When she saw Nazis loading children into trucks she stopped abruptly. The children, babies to eight years old, were frightened and crying.

"When they [the children] did not move fast enough, a Nazi would pick them up by the arm, the leg, or even hair and throw them into the truck," Pritchard remembered. She was so shocked by what she saw that she found herself crying in rage. When two other women tried to stop the loading, the Nazis heaved them into a truck, too.

Marion saw that acting on her anger and confronting the Nazis directly was suicidal. Still, she was forever marked by the events she witnessed and vowed to do something. She found a community in the Dutch underground and started channeling her anger into effective action.

Anger was transformed into love in action. First, she did small acts of defiance by taking food, clothing, and false papers to those in hiding. She also continued her education in social work. This prepared her for the day she arrived at a rendezvous site and was handed a baby. She carried the baby to the delivery house to find the owners had been arrested, so she took responsibility and found another family to care for the baby.

Marion paused, took a step back, and found a way to take a stand. She let her heart break wide open and ultimately saved 150 Dutch Jewish children.

Lynne Twist says, "If you find the stand that you are and the avenue to express it, you can and will move the world."[62]

But even if we find ourselves at a loss, not sure at all what we stand for, we can begin by looking close to home. Maybe we can stand for our children. Maybe we can stand for our dignity at work. Maybe we can stand for a cause we find compelling. Maybe we can stand for enough.

One of our meditation teachers said, "Stay still, allow the breath to anchor you, and be in the moment . . . and if you smell smoke get up and leave because there is probably fire."

Remember love is not meant as an excuse to be delusional or check out. Love is a call to presence, an opportunity to listen deeply to our heart's inner longing and act from that place. Keep standing for life itself. That is where love is.

Love is the source of it all, including our enoughness, and the antidote to hate and fear, which are the breeding grounds for all the forces of scarcity. This seems to be the deepest of the teachings of creating and living within sustainable abundance.

Loving My Enemy

On the tenth anniversary of 9/11, Gina was home after spending six days learning a mindfulness practice called *loving kindness*. She wrote:

> I woke up agitated and found meditation particularly difficult that morning. It occurred to me that maybe the world could use a little more love on this day. I started with my sister, a direct survivor of the attacks on the World Trade Center. Then I sent loving kindness to myself, then a benefactor, friends, and a neutral person.
>
> Then it was time to send loving kindness to my enemy. "Who is my enemy?" I wondered. My mind immediately went to the hijackers. I paused, feeling aversion rise up in my body for a moment. And yet, I was committed to having this new practice be a source of healing on this day. After a moment, I got the courage to send loving kindness to the hijackers, "May you be safe, may you be happy, may you be healthy, may you live with ease."
>
> As I recited the phrases, I felt what could only be described as a melting in my heart. It was as if a piece of my heart that had been frozen for ten years, softened and started to melt. Energy moved and blood flowed into a part of me that I had unknowingly shut off a decade ago. I thought of the hijackers' families, the children they had left behind, the communities that trained them, the people who fed and housed them, the circumstances that brought them to that moment of destruction, the system and context that produced such terror and horror.
>
> I began to understand what it meant to be connected and finished the session by sending loving kindness to all beings. Each and every person, animal or living entity seen or unseen, regardless of crimes committed, perceived value of that being, or even their political persuasion.

Where is the enemy? On one level it seems obvious there are "real" enemies out there. But remember when Solzhenitsyn reminds us that evil cuts through every human heart. Kornfield talks of Gandhi walking from village to village after India was partitioned, and millions had become refugees.[63] The violence was everywhere. Troops went to what was West Pakistan. He went east and asked for the violence to stop. He fasted, refusing to eat again until the violence ceased even if it meant his own death.

Gandhi's actions brought together all of the aspects of love at once. He stood for something larger than his own life. Instead of focusing on what he was against, the perceived enemy, he focused on ending violence itself. Gathering his courage and the force of love, he acted. The potency of his practice, his love, was enough to free a nation.

Do we annihilate the enemy or transform the forces that turn something or someone into the enemy?

True Love

To love another, we must love and cherish this being called "self." To love self, we must know our place and experience belonging to this precious life. To love life, we must remember that we are part of the fabric of everything. It is not possible not to be. To love anyone or anything we must see clearly beyond the veils of scarcity and excess to the piercing truth of enough.

To love we must face our finitude and get humble about our place in this life. We must begin to experience the great rest available when we move out of fighting for everything and into allowing life on life's terms. Love comes from these practices and flows to the center of all things. We are made of love. We are love.

We sometimes say this seventh law is the only law. We are only here for a flicker. So, we ask you: How do you want to spend your "one wild and precious life"?

practices
for law 7

Practice #1:

A Love Inventory

- What is my definition of love?
- How do I know I am being loving?
- How do I know I am being loved?
- Who, what, and where do I love?
- What don't I love or am unwilling to love? And why?
- What practices of love do I have?
- What practices of love would I like to cultivate?
- What would become available if I lived a life of unconditional love?
- Am I willing to start sending love to myself no matter how I am feeling?

Practice #2:

Self-Love Practice: How Well Did I Love Myself This Week?

This is a potent question that you can ask yourself daily or weekly. If you are interested in cultivating certain qualities or letting go of hatred or personal flaws, you can add to the question. For example: How well did I love myself this week? How well did I love my softness, my beauty, my anxiety, and my stubbornness?

Practice #3:

Loving Kindness Meditation

Loving kindness is a practice to cultivate compassion for ourselves and others. It can be a stand-alone meditation practice or be included in your regular mindfulness practice. This can be done at the beginning or end of your formal practice time or every time you find yourself waiting somewhere. With this practice, we find that we are just a little softer, calmer, and less judgmental. We experience compassion not from a place of pity or worry but as a lived experience of balance and connection.

The practice consists of a series of phrases said while in a centered or meditative state. We send a series of "friendly wishes" on behalf of several people, including ourselves. There is a traditional flow, which is outlined below. Following a set structure can provide a strong touch point for developing rhythm and consistency in your practice.

You can do this practice while sitting or walking and out in the world. What's most important is to be settled in a comfortable way and allow the mind to be directed to the intention of sending loving kindness.

THE STRUCTURE OF LOVING KINDNESS
Part I

We start by selecting phrases that resonate with us. We keep the same phrases as we offer our love and kindness outward. Here is a set of four starter phrases:

May I/you be safe.
May I/you be healthy.
May I/you be happy.
May I/you live a life of ease.

Part II

We silently say the phrases to the following people in this order:

- Ourselves
- Benefactor (someone in your life who has mentored you or is a teacher or coach; someone who you know has your back)
- Friends and/or family members and/or work colleagues, perhaps as a group
- Neutral person
- Difficult person
- All beings

Part III

After you get the rhythm of the practices you may want to work with phrases that speak to you more directly. We recommend that you settle on phrases and stick with them for a while. Here are other examples:

May I/you be filled with loving kindness.

May I/you be safe and protected from (inner and outer) harm.

May I/you discover happiness and peace.

May my/your mind and body be healthy and strong.

May my/your body and mind be nourished and cared for.

May I/you find ease and grace.

May my/your heart be full of joy.

May I/you be free from suffering and the causes of suffering.

May I/you be free from danger.

May I/you be free from neglect.

May I/you be free from struggle.

May I/you be free from (fill in the blank, depending on my mood: judgment, self-loathing, fear).

MAKE THIS A DAILY PRACTICE

We encourage you to begin this practice with a commitment to doing it daily for at least a week.

Our clients report this meditation brings them greater ease. One of our clients used loving kindness practice with a particularly difficult direct report. She was struggling with this person and had a lot of judgment about him. This brought up what we might call mental "noise" or inner chatter that ranged from "he is incompetent" to "he wants to sabotage me."

We taught her to practice wishing the person well while she was feeling the strong feelings of frustration, worry, and anger. We asked, "Can you think of at least one thing you could truly wish for him?" She said, "Yes, I can do that."

The instructions were that whenever she felt the judgment or noticed her eyes began to roll, that she would think of a single wish for him and send it. A month later, we checked in with her, because she had not brought up the person that had so dominated our coaching work. "Oh, he's fine now," she said.

We have seen this happen over and over. A client is struggling or suffering and when they do this practice, the problem disappears so profoundly that they often do not recall it ever being an issue.

Practice #4:
Offering Love and Dignity to Those Living on the Street

This is an experiment for those of you who live or work in an urban area and are solicited for money as you are out and about. When asked for money, stop walking and look the person in the eye and greet them.

You can choose to give them something or not and let them know why. Example, "Hello, I am sorry I can't help you today."

You may silently send them some loving kindness, "May you be well."

The key is to look the person in the eye and acknowledge them as a fellow traveler on our collective journey.

One caveat: If the person is showing signs of mental instability then looking them in the eye could be too stimulating for them. In that case, silently wish loving kindness as you move past them.

Practice #5:
Offering Love at Work

Experiment with bringing love to work (customized to your environment). This is an opportunity for you to bring love, without conditions, to your customers, coworkers, managers, senior leadership, and all support staff, including the janitorial and maintenance staff. Here are some ideas for this experiment:

- Bring an attitude of love and gratitude to everyone and every meeting for a week and notice if your experience of work changes.
- Have lunch with someone from another department or who is at a very different level in the organization. You could do this monthly and at the end of the year have connected to twelve new people.
- Every day for a month, acknowledge a different person for a job well done; this experiment ensures you acknowledged twenty different stakeholders.

- Check in: Before starting your regular meeting, ask everyone to check in to see how they are doing.
- Check out: When completing a meeting, have everyone offer an appreciation.
- As part of your regular practice, have the courage to ask any stakeholder the following:
  - What brought you to our organization?
  - What do you love about working here?
  - What do you love about your job?
  - How does your work align with your passion?
  - What are your hopes and dreams for the future? How does this job, role, company fulfill your dream?

Practice #6:
Imagining a Sufficient World

As Oscar Hammerstein II wrote in the musical *South Pacific*, "You got to have a dream. If you don't have a dream, how you gonna have a dream come true?"

We'll use this final practice to imagine our dream world, in as much detail as we can.

Take a few easy deep breaths. When you're ready, close your eyes. Imagine for a moment a world that is sufficient, sustainable, and abundant. *Enough for all.*

Start with yourself: How do you look and feel? What are your days like? What is your place in the world? Who are the people surrounding you?

What's happening in this world? Have a look around. Take a walk down the street. Check out all the different institutions: your local schools, your town, city, or state government.

In this world what does the federal government care about? How do we, as a nation, spend our money? In your imagination, what do corporations have their attention on? How about the nonprofit sector? Have any of them vanished or been transformed? How?

What is happening in marriage and family structures, social services? How are laws being made and enforced? Notice and include all the helping professions, all the people who come to our rescue when there's a fire or an altercation that needs support from those in uniform.

How do we make maps in a sufficient world? Where are the lines drawn? Are they drawn at all? Is there a new way of experiencing nationalism or a new way of experiencing our identity? How does that look in practice?

What does our food supply look like? If we traced the seed all the way to the table, all those interactions, the way we grocery shop, the way we interact with those who grow our food, our favorite restaurants, how would we be treating each other?

What interactions and changes do we see around us? How is the media affected? Keep imagining. Keep looking. If there's a place that's dark or just blank or you can't quite see clearly, just breathe there. It might not be clear yet. If there are other places that are crystal clear, keep crystallizing them.

Then follow the thread to another institution, another entity. How would modern life be different? Some of you are poets and activists, musicians and artists. Paint or sing or write of this world.

When you're done imagining and dreaming you may want to write it down, draw it, collage it, give it some form. Then make it a practice to keep dreaming, keep imagining those interactions, those rich exchanges between people, institutions, organizations, sectors, industries. Keep imagining it. Bring it forth.

notes

1   Annie Leonard, in a keynote address at the 2010 Bioneers by the Bay Conference in Bedford, MA.

2   David Loy, *Insight Journal* interview, Upaya Newsletter, April 5, 2010, https://www.upaya.org/newsletter/view/2010/04/05#story13.

3   John Monczunski, "Spent," *Notre Dame Magazine*. March 26, 2004.

4   Scott Pape, "The Engagement Ring: One of the Biggest Marketing Conjobs in History," "The Barefoot Investor," HeraldSun.com.au, September 16, 2016, http://www.heraldsun.com.au/business/barefoot-investor/the-engagement -ring-one-of-the-biggest-marketing-conjobs-in-history/news-story/35ac8bd 4dcca569305e94a232298213a.

5   Lynne Twist, *The Soul of Money: Transforming Your Relationship with Money and Life* (New York: W. W. Norton, 2010).

6   Edith Zimmerman, "Oliver Burkeman and the Pursuit of Happiness," on TheHairpin.com. November 13, 2012.

7   Twist, *The Soul of Money.*

8   *Planetary,* directed by Guy Reid and Steve Watts Kennedy, distributed by Sunfilm Entertainment and Tiberis Films, 2015.

9   Christopher Chabris and Daniel Simons, *The Invisible Gorilla: How Our Intuitions Deceive Us* (New York: Crown Books, 2010).

10 Twist, *The Soul of Money.*

11 Matthew Budd and Larry Rothstein (New York: Three Rivers Press), 124–26.

12 Krista Tippett, "Where Does it Hurt?" from the podcast *On Being*, August 17, 2017, https://onbeing.org/programs/ruby-sales-where-does -it-hurt-aug2017/.

13 Richard Strozzi-Heckler, *Holding the Center: Sanctuary in a Time of Confusion* (Berkeley, CA: Frog Books, 1997).

14 Joseph Goldstein and Jack Kornfield, *Seeking the Heart of Wisdom: The Path of Insight Meditation* (Boston: Shambhala, 1987), 3.

15 Marlene Schiwy, *A Voice of Her Own: Women and the Journal-Writing Journey* (New York: Simon & Schuster, 1996), 204.

16 Jon Kabat-Zinn, *Wherever You Go, There You Are: Mindfulness Meditation in Everyday Life* (New York: Hyperion, 1994).

17 David Whyte, *The House of Belonging* (Langley, WA: Many Rivers Press, 1997), 4.

18 Fritjof Capra, *Hidden Connections* (New York: Doubleday, 2002), 152.

19 Sebastian Junger, *Tribe: On Homecoming and Belonging* (New York: Twelve, 2016).

20 Brooke Gladstone, "#3: Rags to Riches," *On the Media*, October 13, 2016.

21 Helena Norberg-Hodge, *Ancient Futures: Learning from Ladakh* (San Francisco, CA: Sierra Club Books, 1991).

22 Unsettling America, "We Were All Indigenous and Can Again Become," UnsettlingAmerica.com, May 26, 2011, https://unsettlingamerica.word-press.com/2011/05/26/we-were-all-indigenous-and-can-again-become/.

23 Sharon Salzberg, *Loving-Kindness: The Revolutionary Art of Happiness* (Boston: Shambhala, 2008), 106.

24 Matthew Lieberman, *Social: Why Our Brains Are Wired to Connect* (New York: Crown, 2013).

25 Daniel Siegel, *Mindsight: The New Science of Personal Transformation* (New York: Random House, 2010).

26 Thomas Lewis, Fari Amini, and Richard Lannon, *A General Theory of Love* (New York: Knopf Doubleday, 2007), 85.

27 Martin Luther King, Jr., "Remaining Awake through a Great Revolution," 1965 Oberlin College commencement address, http://www2.oberlin .edu/external/EOG/BlackHistoryMonth/MLK/CommAddress.html.

28 Gene Baur with George Stone, *Living the Farm Sanctuary Life* (New York: Rodale, 2015), 88.

29 Jack Kornfield, *Bringing Home the Dharma: Awakening Right Where You Are* (Boston: Shambhala, 2011), 26.

30 South African Sesotho poem, read by Afrikaner poet Antjie Krog in her speech "African Forgiveness—Too Sophisticated for the West" at the International Literature Festival Berlin, September 21, 2004, http://www .literaturfestival.com/intern/reden/krog-engl.

31 United Nations General Assembly resolution 217A, in the Universal Declaration of Human Rights, adopted at the third session of the United Nations General Assembly in Paris, France, on December 10, 1948.

32 *The Best Exotic Marigold Hotel*, directed by John Madden (Century City, CA: Fox Searchlight, 2012), DVD.

33 Mary Oliver, "When Death Comes," *New and Selected Poems*, vol. 1 (Boston, MA: Beacon Press, 1992), 10.

34 George Leonard, *Mastery: The Keys to Success and Long-Term Fulfillment* (New York: Penguin, 1992).

35 William Bridges, *Managing Transitions: Making the Most of Change* (London: Hodder & Stoughton, 2011).

36 The Nonviolent Communication website is https://www.cnvc.org/.

37 Richard Boyzatis and Annie McKee, *Resonant Leadership: Renewing Yourself and Connecting with Others through Mindfulness, Hope, and Compassion* (Boston, MA: Harvard Business Review Press).

38 Bhikkhu Bodhi, ed., *In the Buddha's Words: An Anthology of Discourses from the Pali Canon* (Somerville, MA: Wisdom Publications, 2005), 32.

39 Translated as both the second "arrow" or "dart." *In the Buddha's Words*, 31.

40 Jalal ad-Din Muhammad Rumi, Coleman Barks, trans., "A Great Wagon," *The Essential Rumi,* New Expanded Edition (New York: Harper Collins, 2010), 35.

41 Viktor Frankl, *Man's Search for Meaning* (Boston: Beacon Press, 2015).

42 Van Jones, speaking at the Pachamama Alliance symposium "Awakening the Dreamer Changing the Dream," https://www.pachamama.org/engage/awakening-the-dreamer.

43 Alan Rosenblith, *The Money Fix*, directed by Alan Rosenblith, 2009, DVD.

44 Frankl, *Man's Search for Meaning.*

45 Rabbi Earl A. Grollman, "When Life Gives You Death, What Is So Funny?" blog post by Fran Smith and Sheila Himmel, PsychologyToday .com, January 2014, https://www.psychologytoday.com/blog/changing -the-way-we-die/201401/when-life-gives-you-death-whats-so-funny.

46 The Dalai Lama, *My Spiritual Journey* (New York: Harper Collins, 2011), 23.

47 Lee Berk and Stanley Tan, "Cortisol and Catecholamine Stress Hormone Decrease Is Associated with the Behavior of Perceptual Anticipation of Mirthful Laughter," Loma Linda, CA: Oak Crest Health Research Institute, http://www.the-aps.org/mm/hp/Audiences/Public-Press/Archive/08/10.html.

48 Norman Cousins, *Anatomy of an Illness as Perceived by the Patient: Reflections on Healing and Regeneration* (Open Road Media, 2016).

49 Diane Coutu, "How Resilience Works," *Harvard Business Review* May 2002.

50 Alexis de Tocqueville, Harvey Mansfield and Delba Winthrop, trans., *Democracy in America* (Chicago: University of Chicago Press, 2002).

51 Douglas Abrams, *The Book of Joy: Lasting Happiness in a Changing World* (New York: Penguin, 2016).

52 Kornfield, *Bringing Home the Dharma.*

53 Thich Nhat Hanh, *Peace Is Every Step: The Path of Mindfulness in Everyday Life* (New York: Bantam Books, 1991), 21.

54 Abrams, *The Book of Joy.*

55 Mahatma Gandhi, *The Essential Writings* (Oxford University Press, 2008), 61.

56 Aleksandr Solzhenitsyn, *The Gulag Archipelago* (New York: Harper Collins, 2007).

57 Salzberg, *Loving-Kindness,* 108.

58 Tara Brach, "Awakening from the Trance of Unworthiness," *Inquiring Mind* 17, no. 2 (Spring 2001).

59 Emma Varvaloucas, "Q&A with Thirty-Year Vipassana Instructor Michele McDonald," *Tricycle,* July 21, 2011.

60 Lynne Twist, personal communication to Gina LaRoche during Twist's course "Fundraising from the Heart," New York City, February 12–13, 2015.

61 Eva Fogelman, *Conscience and Courage: Rescuers of Jews during the Holocaust* (New York: Anchor Books, 1994).

62 Lynne Twist, personal communication.

63 Kornfield, *Bringing Home the Dharma.*

acknowledgments

We would like to thank our original Boston Sufficiency community: Carol Dearborn, Miriam Hawley, Bill Kennedy, Bill Kistler, Martha Russell, Kristi Scarpone, Michael Scarpone, Rosemary Tator, and Wes Tator. Our work with the Seven Laws was born in that community. We love you all. Thank you for who you are and for your longing for a world that supports all life thriving.

The notion that this work could be expressed in the pages of a book began with our agent Linda Loewenthal. Thank you, Linda, for your clear seeing and for holding the long view. We would also like to thank Shea Adelson, the first person to join Seven Stones. We often called Shea "our Velveteen Rabbit." She was the little boy in the story who made the rabbit come to life through his love. Shea kept inviting us to see what we had to offer as more and more real. And more than that, she toiled many hours working on early proposals and an early book pitch. Shea, you are in the DNA of the work and of the book. Thank you. Eileen, you have been with us since the beginning in a variety of ways. In relationship to this book you have been a fierce and loving editor, standing for us getting clear on our message in every way. Thank you for everything you gave to make this book come to life.

Debra Ollivier, on the recommendation of our dear friend and colleague Pattie Belle Hastings, introduced us to Parallax Press. We want to thank the entire team at Parallax, especially publisher Rachel Neumann. Our editor, Daniel Will-Harris, had the vision to get our thoughts and ideas into a cohesive structure. We don't know if we would have ever finished the manuscript without his steady hand.

Thank you to Sue Richardson, Jennifer Krier, Cathie Desjardin, and Pema Teeter. Your comments kept us sane and pointed us to the book's true north. Anna Sternoff helped us hone the voice of Seven Stones. Kim Hunley, Stacy Blake-Beard, and Cheryl LaRoche: thank you for being part of Gina's writing group for over ten years. Thank you, Cheryl, for your extra heroic effort as this book went to press.

Finally, to all of the Seven Stones community and to our clients past, present, and future, thank you for the opportunity to stand with and for all of our lives. Our liberation is bound up together. Until we are all home, no one is home. It is our profound honor to walk with you. To all those who have our backs at Seven Stones: Becky, Kate, Kelly, Viv, Michelle, and Emma. You are the women behind the women. "Thank you" does not begin to convey the gratitude we have for your incredible support. To our growing family of colleagues and coaches, and to our inaugural cohort of incredible graduates, we are so blessed to be in community with you all. Thank you for who you are and for your stand for life.

Finally, we would like to thank and acknowledge a few people individually.

Jen: My life has been a guided journey back home to myself. I'd like to acknowledge the people who showed me the light through some very dark tunnels. First, Adrianne Mohr. You pulled me back from the depths of hell and sent me into the arms of two incredibly gifted teachers: Richard Strozzi Heckler and Robert Hall. The three of you collectively saved my life and put me squarely on a path to being the person who could write this book. Sonika Tinker, you inspired me to become a passionate coach and a loving human being. The foundation you four amazing beings provided me is priceless. I am forever in your debt. I cannot express enough gratitude to all of the clients and students I have had over the last almost thirty years now. You have taught me so much about the path home. It's an honor and a privilege to stand with and for you—to walk hand in hand toward a world that is sustainable and sustaining and to see clearly the bounty offered by life. life. To Amy Fox: you have for so long been a stand for my greatness. Thank you for that and for providing environments for me to make visible what you have seen all along. I love you.

To my family: First, my family of origin—my greatest teachers about life, about pain, about love, about humility, and about forgiveness. To John Rice, my husband, the strong oak against which I get to rest, and Sophia Stella Rebecca, my daughter: thank you for your hearts and your steady home. You remind me every day why I do this work, why our lives matter, why we must call forth a world of sustainable abundance. Sophia and Griffin and Jackson, may this book make but a small difference in the lives you get to live after we are gone. Finally, to Gina: These last ten years of partnering with you has been a gift from the Gods. You are an amazing human being and you make me a better one. Thank you from the bottom of my heart for playing so full out, and for your unconditional love. Our partnership is one of the great blessings of my life.

Gina: I would like to acknowledge my parents, Cheryl and Calvin LaRoche, and my dear sisters who hold me close, Renee LaRoche-Morris and Danielle King. Thank you to my menfolk, my sons Jackson and Griffin, who have emerged as amazing young men, creating their lives from sustainable abundance. Finally, thank you to my husband, Alan Price. Words are inadequate to express my love and gratitude for all you have done to support me, Seven Stones, and making of this book. Thank you, thank you, thank you. YLW.

about the authors

Gina LaRoche is cofounder of Seven Stones Leadership Group and a leading organizational consultant, executive coach, speaker, author, and artist. She is noted for executive programs that challenge leaders, teams, and entrepreneurs to accelerate results and develop mindfulness and presence for themselves and their organizations. A popular keynote speaker, Gina is a graduate of Spirit Rock's Community Dharma Leaders Program and a board member of Insight Meditation Society. She holds a BSBA from Georgetown University and an MBA from Harvard Business School.

Jennifer Cohen is cofounder of Seven Stones Leadership Group and an engaging speaker and author, well known for coaching world-class leaders from institutions, including Harvard Business School and Simmons. Quantum physics, ontology, neuroscience, somatics, and systems thinking inform her innovative and embodied approaches to curriculum design and facilitation. She holds a master's degree in applied psychology from the Antioch New England Graduate School and is certified as a Master Somatic Coach by the Strozzi Institute.

message to readers

As stewards of the Sustainable Abundance movement, we appreciate your listening for a new, empowering context. You too can live a life of enough.

We aim to relentlessly debunk society's scarcity myths and provide you an antidote to anxiety, fear, distraction, and shame. Know that we all have, do, and are enough—including you.

Living a life of enough is a moment-to-moment practice of being present and receptive to the bounty everywhere. Join us.

Gina LaRoche and Jennifer Cohen
www.sevenstonesleadership.com

related
titles

The Art of Money, Bari Tessler
Awakening Joy, James Baraz and Shoshana Alexander
The Mindful Athlete, George Mumford
Ocean of Insight, Heather Lyn Mann
Work, Thich Nhat Hanh
Work That Matters, Maia Duerr

PARALLAX
PRESS

Parallax Press, a nonprofit publisher founded by Zen Master Thich Nhat Hanh, publishes books and media on the art of mindful living and Engaged Buddhism. We are committed to offering teachings that help transform suffering and injustice. Our aspiration is to contribute to collective insight and awakening, bringing about a more joyful, healthy, and compassionate society.

For a copy of the catalog, please contact:

Parallax Press
P.O. Box 7355
Berkeley, CA 94707
parallax.org